The Faerie Queene by Edmund Spenser

Book V. The Legend of Artegall

THE FIFTH BOOKE OF THE FAERIE QUEENE CONTAYNING THE LEGEND OF ARTEGALL OR OF JUSTICE

One of the greatest of English poets, Edmund Spenser was born in East Smithfield, London, in 1552. He was educated in London at the Merchant Taylors' School and later at Pembroke College, Cambridge. In 1579, he published The Shepheardes Calender, his first major work.

Edmund journeyed to Ireland in July 1580, in the service of the newly appointed Lord Deputy, Arthur Grey, 14th Baron Grey de Wilton. His time included the terrible massacre at the Siege of Smerwick.

The epic poem, The Faerie Queene, is acknowledged as Edmund's masterpiece. The first three books were published in 1590, and a second set of three books were published in 1596.

Indeed the reality is that Spenser, through his great talents, was able to move Poetry in a different direction. It led to him being called a Poet's Poet and brought rich admiration from Milton, Raleigh, Blake, Wordsworth, Keats, Byron, and Lord Tennyson, among others.

Spenser returned to Ireland and in 1591, Complaints, a collection of poems that voices complaints in mournful or mocking tones was published.

In 1595, Spenser published Amoretti and Epithalamion. The volume contains eighty-nine sonnets.

In the following year Spenser wrote a prose pamphlet titled A View of the Present State of Ireland, a highly inflammatory argument for the pacification and destruction of Irish culture.

On January 13th 1599 Edmund Spenser died at the age of forty-six. His coffin was carried to his grave in Westminster Abbey by other poets, who threw many pens and pieces of poetry into his grave followed with many tears.

Index of Contents
Book V. The Legend of Artegall
Introductory Verses
Canto I
Canto II
Canto III
Canto IV
Canto V
Canto VI
Canto VII
Canto VIII
Canto IX
Canto X
Canto XI
Canto XII
Edmund Spenser – A Short Biography
Edmund Spenser – A Concise Bibliography

INTRODUCTORY VERSES

I
So oft as I with state of present time
The image of the antique world compare,
When as mans age was in his freshest prime,
And the first blossome of faire vertue bare,
Such oddes I finde twixt those, and these which are,
As that, through long continuance of his course,
Me seemes the world is runne quite out of square
From the first point of his appointed sourse,
And being once amisse, growes daily wourse and wourse.

II
For from the golden age, that first was named,
It's now at earst become a stonie one;
And men themselves, the which at first were framed
Of earthly mould, and form'd of flesh and bone,
Are now transformed into hardest stone:
Such as behind their backs (so backward bred)
Were throwne by Pyrrha and Deucalione:
And if then those may any worse be red,
They into that ere long will be degendered.

III
Let none then blame me, if in discipline
Of vertue and of civill uses lore,
I doe not forme them to the common line
Of present dayes, which are corrupted sore,
But to the antique use which was of yore,
When good was onely for it selfe desyred,
And all men sought their owne, and none no more;
When Justice was not for most meed outhyred,
But simple Truth did rayne, and was of all admyred.

IV
For that which all men then did vertue call
Is now cald vice; and that which vice was hight,
Is now hight vertue, and so us'd of all:
Right now is wrong, and wrong that was is right,
As all things else in time are chaunged quight.
Ne wonder; for the heavens revolution
Is wandred farre from where it first was pight,
And so doe make contrarie constitution
Of all this lower world, toward his dissolution.

V
For who so list into the heavens looke,

And search the courses of the rowling spheares,
Shall find that from the point where they first tooke
Their setting forth, in these few thousand yeares
They all are wandred much; that plaine appeares.
For that same golden fleecy Ram, which bore
Phrixus and Helle from their stepdames feares,
Hath now forgot where he was plast of yore,
And shouldred hath the Bull, which fayre Europa bore.

VI
And eke the Bull hath with his bow-bent horne
So hardly butted those two Twinnes of Jove,
That they have crusht the Crab, and quite him borne
Into the great Nemœan Lions grove.
So now all range, and doe at randon rove
Out of their proper places farre away,
And all this world with them amisse doe move,
And all his creatures from their course astray,
Till they arrive at their last ruinous decay.

VII
Ne is that same great glorious lampe of light,
That doth enlumine all these lesser fyres,
In better case, ne keepes his course more right,
But is miscaried with the other spheres.
For since the terme of fourteene hundred yeres,
That learned Ptolomæe his hight did take,
He is declyned from that marke of theirs
Nigh thirtie minutes to the southerne lake;
That makes me feare in time he will us quite forsake.

VIII
And if to those Ægyptian wisards old,
Which in star-read were wont have best insight,
Faith may be given, it is by them told,
That since the time they first tooke the sunnes hight,
Foure times his place he shifted hath in sight,
And twice hath risen where he now doth west,
And wested twice where he ought rise aright.
But most is Mars amisse of all the rest,
And next to him old Saturne, that was wont be best.

IX
For during Saturnes ancient raigne it's sayd
That all the world with goodnesse did abound:
All loved vertue, no man was affrayd
Of force, ne fraud in wight was to be found:
No warre was knowne, no dreadfull trompets sound,
Peace universall rayn'd mongst men and beasts,
And all things freely grew out of the ground:
Justice sate high ador'd with solemne feasts,

And to all people did divide her dred beheasts.

X
Most sacred vertue she of all the rest,
Resembling God in his imperiall might;
Whose soveraine powre is herein most exprest,
That both to good and bad he dealeth right,
And all his workes with justice hath bedight.
That powre he also doth to princes lend,
And makes them like himselfe in glorious sight,
To sit in his owne seate, his cause to end,
And rule his people right, as he doth recommend.

XI
Dread soverayne goddesse, that doest highest sit
In seate of judgement, in th' Almighties stead,
And with magnificke might and wondrous wit
Doest to thy people righteous doome aread,
That furthest nations filles with awfull dread,
Pardon the boldnesse of thy basest thrall,
That dare discourse of so divine a read,
As thy great justice praysed over all:
The instrument whereof, loe! here thy Artegall.

CANTO I

Artegall trayn'd in Justice lore
Irenaes quest pursewed;
He doeth avenge on Sanglier
His ladies bloud embrewed.

I
Though vertue then were held in highest price,
In those old times of which I doe intreat,
Yet then likewise the wicked seede of vice
Began to spring; which shortly grew full great,
And with their boughes the gentle plants did beat.
But evermore some of the vertuous race
Rose up, inspired with heroicke heat,
That cropt the branches of the sient base,
And with strong hand their fruitfull rancknes did deface.

II
Such first was Bacchus, that with furious might
All th' East, before untam'd, did overronne,
And wrong repressed, and establish right,
Which lawlesse men had formerly fordonne:

There Justice first her princely rule begonne.
Next Hercules his like ensample shewed,
Who all the West with equall conquest wonne,
And monstrous tyrants with his club subdewed;
The club of Justice dread, with kingly powre endewed.

III
And such was he of whom I have to tell,
The champion of true Justice, Artegall:
Whom (as ye lately mote remember well)
An hard adventure, which did then befall,
Into redoubted perill forth did call;
That was to succour a distressed dame,
Whom a strong tyrant did unjustly thrall,
And from the heritage which she did clame
Did with strong hand withhold: Grantorto was his name.

IV
Wherefore the lady, which Eirena hight,
Did to the Faery Queene her way addresse,
To whom complayning her afflicted plight,
She her besought of gratious redresse.
That soveraine queene, that mightie emperesse,
Whose glorie is to aide all suppliants pore,
And of weake princes to be patronesse,
Chose Artegall to right her to restore;
For that to her he seem'd best skild in righteous lore.

V
For Artegall in justice was upbrought
Even from the cradle of his infancie,
And all the depth of rightfull doome was taught
By faire Astræa, with great industrie,
Whilest here on earth she lived mortallie.
For till the world from his perfection fell
Into all filth and foule iniquitie,
Astræa here mongst earthly men did dwell,
And in the rules of justice them instructed well.

VI
Whiles through the world she walked in this sort,
Upon a day she found this gentle childe,
Amongst his peres playing his childish sport:
Whom seeing fit, and with no crime defilde,
She did allure with gifts and speaches milde
To wend with her. So thence him farre she brought
Into a cave from companie exilde,
In which she noursled him, till yeares he raught,
And all the discipline of justice there him taught.

VII

There she him taught to weigh both right and wrong
In equall ballance with due recompence,
And equitie to measure out along,
According to the line of conscience,
When so it needs with rigour to dispence.
Of all the which, for want there of mankind,
She caused him to make experience
Upon wyld beasts, which she in woods did find,
With wrongfull powre oppressing others of their kind.

VIII
Thus she him trayned, and thus she him taught,
In all the skill of deeming wrong and right,
Untill the ripenesse of mans yeares he raught;
That even wilde beasts did feare his awfull sight,
And men admyr'd his overruling might;
Ne any liv'd on ground, that durst withstand
His dreadfull heast, much lesse him match in fight,
Or bide the horror of his wreakfull hand,
When so he list in wrath lift up his steely brand.

IX
Which steely brand, to make him dreaded more,
She gave unto him, gotten by her slight
And earnest search, where it was kept in store
In Joves eternall house, unwist of wight,
Since he himselfe it us'd in that great fight
Against the Titans, that whylome rebelled
Gainst highest heaven; Chrysaor it was hight;
Chrysaor that all other swords excelled,
Well prov'd in that same day, when Jove those gyants quelled.

X
For of most perfect metall it was made,
Tempred with adamant amongst the same,
And garnisht all with gold upon the blade
In goodly wise, whereof it tooke his name,
And was of no lesse vertue then of fame:
For there no substance was so firme and hard,
But it would pierce or cleave, where so it came;
Ne any armour could his dint out ward;
But wheresoever it did light, it throughly shard.

XI
Now when the world with sinne gan to abound,
Astræa loathing lenger here to space
Mongst wicked men, in whom no truth she found,
Return'd to heaven, whence she deriv'd her race;
Where she hath now an everlasting place,
Mongst those twelve signes which nightly we doe see
The heavens bright-shining baudricke to enchace;

And is the Virgin, sixt in her degree,
And next her selfe her righteous ballance hanging bee.

XII
But when she parted hence, she left her groome,
An yron man, which did on her attend
Alwayes, to execute her stedfast doome,
And willed him with Artegall to wend,
And doe what ever thing he did intend.
His name was Talus, made of yron mould,
Immoveable, resistlesse, without end;
Who in his hand an yron flale did hould,
With which he thresht out falshood, and did truth unfould.

XIII
He now went with him in this new inquest,
Him for to aide, if aide he chaunst to neede,
Against that cruell tyrant, which opprest
The faire Irena with his foule misdeede,
And kept the crowne in which she should succeed.
And now together on their way they bin,
When as they saw a squire in squallid weed,
Lamenting sore his sorowfull sad tyne,
With many bitter teares shed from his blubbred eyne.

XIV
To whom as they approched, they espide
A sorie sight, as ever seene with eye;
An headlesse ladie lying him beside,
In her owne blood all wallow'd wofully,
That her gay clothes did in discolour die.
Much was he moved at that ruefull sight;
And flam'd with zeale of vengeance inwardly,
He askt who had that dame so fouly dight;
Or whether his owne hand, or whether other wight?

XV
'Ah, woe is me, and well away!' quoth hee,
Bursting forth teares, like springs out of a banke,
'That ever I this dismall day did see!
Full farre was I from thinking such a pranke;
Yet litle losse it were, and mickle thanke,
If I should graunt that I have doen the same,
That I mote drinke the cup whereof she dranke:
But that I should die guiltie of the blame,
The which another did, who now is fled with shame.'

XVI
'Who was it then,' sayd Artegall, 'that wrought?
And why? doe it declare unto me trew.'
'A knight,' said he, 'if knight he may be thought,

That did his hand in ladies bloud embrew,
And for no cause, but as I shall you shew.
This day as I in solace sate hereby
With a fayre love, whose losse I now do rew,
There came this knight, having in companie
This lucklesse ladie, which now here doth headlesse lie.

XVII
'He, whether mine seem'd fayrer in his eye,
Or that he wexed weary of his owne,
Would change with me; but I did it denye;
So did the ladies both, as may be knowne:
But he, whose spirit was with pride upblowne,
Would not so rest contented with his right,
But having from his courser her downe throwne,
Fro me reft mine away by lawlesse might,
And on his steed her set, to beare her out of sight.

XVIII
'Which when his ladie saw, she follow'd fast,
And on him catching hold, gan loud to crie
Not so to leave her, nor away to cast,
But rather of his hand besought to die.
With that his sword he drew all wrathfully,
And at one stroke cropt off her head with scorne,
In that same place whereas it now doth lie.
So he my love away with him hath borne,
And left me here, both his and mine owne love to morne.'

XIX
'Aread,' sayd he, 'which way then did he make?
And by what markes may he be knowne againe?'
'To hope,' quoth he, 'him soone to overtake,
That hence so long departed, is but vaine:
But yet he pricked over yonder plaine,
And as I marked, bore upon his shield,
By which it's easie him to know againe,
A broken sword within a bloodie field;
Expressing well his nature, which the same did wield.'

XX
No sooner sayd, but streight he after sent
His yron page, who him pursew'd so light,
As that it seem'd above the ground he went:
For he was swift as swallow in her flight,
And strong as lyon in his lordly might.
It was not long before he overtooke
Sir Sanglier (so cleeped was that knight);
Whom at the first he ghessed by his looke,
And by the other markes which of his shield he tooke.

XXI
He bad him stay, and backe with him retire;
Who, full of scorne to be commaunded so,
The lady to alight did eft require,
Whilest he reformed that uncivill fo:
And streight at him with all his force did go.
Who mov'd no more therewith, then when a rocke
Is lightly stricken with some stones throw;
But to him leaping, lent him such a knocke,
That on the ground he layd him like a sencelesse blocke.

XXII
But ere he could him selfe recure againe,
Him in his iron paw he seized had;
That when he wak't out of his warelesse paine,
He found him selfe, unwist, so ill bestad,
That lim he could not wag. Thence he him lad,
Bound like a beast appointed to the stall:
The sight whereof the lady sore adrad,
And fain'd to fly for feare of being thrall;
But he her quickly stayd, and forst to wend withall.

XXIII
When to the place they came, where Artegall
By that same carefull squire did then abide,
He gently gan him to demaund of all,
That did betwixt him and that squire betide.
Who with sterne countenance and indignant pride
Did aunswere, that of all he guiltlesse stood,
And his accuser thereuppon defide:
For neither he did shed that ladies bloud,
Nor tooke away his love, but his owne proper good.

XXIV
Well did the squire perceive him selfe too weake,
To aunswere his defiaunce in the field,
And rather chose his challenge off to breake,
Then to approve his right with speare and shield,
And rather guilty chose him selfe to yield.
But Artegall by signes perceiving plaine
That he it was not which that lady kild,
But that strange knight, the fairer love to gaine,
Did cast about by sleight the truth thereout to straine;

XXV
And sayd: 'Now sure this doubtfull causes right
Can hardly but by sacrament be tride,
Or else by ordele, or by blooddy fight;
That ill perhaps mote fall to either side.
But if ye please that I your cause decide,
Perhaps I may all further quarrell end,

So ye will sweare my judgement to abide.'
Thereto they both did franckly condiscend,
And to his doome with listfull eares did both attend.

XXVI
'Sith then,' sayd he, 'ye both the dead deny,
And both the living lady claime your right,
Let both the dead and living equally
Devided be betwixt you here in sight,
And each of either take his share aright.
But looke, who does dissent from this my read,
He for a twelve moneths day shall in despight
Beare for his penaunce that same ladies head;
To witnesse to the world that she by him is dead.'

XXVII
Well pleased with that doome was Sangliere,
And offred streight the lady to be slaine.
But that same squire, to whom she was more dere,
When as he saw she should be cut in twaine,
Did yield, she rather should with him remaine
Alive, then to him selfe be shared dead;
And rather then his love should suffer paine,
He chose with shame to beare that ladies head.
True love despiseth shame, when life is cald in dread.

XXVIII
Whom when so willing Artegall perceaved,
'Not so, thou squire,' he sayd, 'but thine I deeme
The living lady, which from thee he reaved:
For worthy thou of her doest rightly seeme.
And you, sir knight, that love so light esteeme,
As that ye would for little leave the same,
Take here your owne, that doth you best beseeme,
And with it beare the burden of defame;
Your owne dead ladies head, to tell abrode your shame.'

XXIX
But Sangliere disdained much his doome,
And sternly gan repine at his beheast;
Ne would for ought obay, as did become,
To beare that ladies head before his breast:
Untill that Talus had his pride represt,
And forced him, maulgre, it up to reare.
Who when he saw it bootelesse to resist,
He tooke it up, and thence with him did beare,
As rated spaniell takes his burden up for feare.

XXX
Much did that squire Sir Artegall adore,
For his great justice, held in high regard;

And as his squire him offred evermore
To serve, for want of other meete reward,
And wend with him on his adventure hard.
But he thereto would by no meanes consent;
But leaving him, forth on his journey far'd:
Ne wight with him but onely Talus went;
They two enough t' encounter an whole regiment.

CANTO II

Artegall heares of Florimell;
Does with the Pagan fight:
Him slaies, drownes Lady Munera,
Does race her castle quight.

I

Nought is more honorable to a knight,
Ne better doth beseeme brave chevalry,
Then to defend the feeble in their right,
And wrong redresse in such as wend awry.
Whilome those great heroes got thereby
Their greatest glory, for their rightfull deedes,
And place deserved with the gods on hy.
Herein the noblesse of this knight exceedes,
Who now to perils great for justice sake proceedes.

II

To which as he now was uppon the way,
He chaunst to meet a dwarfe in hasty course;
Whom he requir'd his forward hast to stay,
Till he of tidings mote with him discourse.
Loth was the dwarfe, yet did he stay perforse,
And gan of sundry newes his store to tell,
As to his memory they had recourse:
But chiefely of the fairest Florimell,
How she was found againe, and spousde to Marinell.

III

For this was Dony, Florimels owne dwarfe,
Whom having lost (as ye have heard whyleare)
And finding in the way the scattred scarfe,
The fortune of her life long time did feare.
But of her health when Artegall did heare,
And safe returne, he was full inly glad,
And askt him where and when her bridale cheare
Should be solemniz'd: for if time he had,
He would be there, and honor to her spousall ad.

IV
'Within three daies,' quoth he, 'as I do here,
It will be at the Castle of the Strond;
What time, if naught me let, I will be there
To doe her service, so as I am bond.
But in my way a little here beyond
A cursed cruell Sarazin doth wonne,
That keepes a bridges passage by strong hond,
And many errant knights hath there fordonne;
That makes all men for feare that passage for to shonne.'

V
'What mister wight,' quoth he, 'and how far hence
Is he, that doth to travellers such harmes?'
'He is,' said he, 'a man of great defence;
Expert in battell and in deedes of armes;
And more emboldned by the wicked charmes,
With which his daughter doth him still support;
Having great lordships got and goodly farmes,
Through strong oppression of his powre extort;
By which he stil them holds, and keepes with strong effort.

VI
'And dayly he his wrongs encreaseth more;
For never wight he lets to passe that way,
Over his bridge, albee he rich or poore,
But he him makes his passage-penny pay:
Else he doth hold him backe or beat away.
Thereto he hath a groome of evill guize,
Whose scalp is bare, that bondage doth bewray,
Which pols and pils the poore in piteous wize;
But he him selfe uppon the rich doth tyrannize.

VII
'His name is hight Pollente, rightly so,
For that he is so puissant and strong,
That with his powre he all doth overgo,
And makes them subject to his mighty wrong;
And some by sleight he eke doth underfong:
For on a bridge he custometh to fight,
Which is but narrow, but exceeding long;
And in the same are many trap fals pight,
Through which the rider downe doth fall through oversight.

VIII
'And underneath the same a river flowes,
That is both swift and dangerous deepe withall;
Into the which whom so he overthrowes,
All destitute of helpe doth headlong fall;
But he him selfe, through practise usuall,

Leapes forth into the floud, and there assaies
His foe confused through his sodaine fall,
That horse and man he equally dismaies,
And either both them drownes, or trayterously slaies.

IX
'Then doth he take the spoile of them at will,
And to his daughter brings, that dwels thereby:
Who all that comes doth take, and therewith fill
The coffers of her wicked threasury;
Which she with wrongs hath heaped up so hy,
That many princes she in wealth exceedes,
And purchast all the countrey lying ny
With the revenue of her plenteous meedes:
Her name is Munera, agreeing with her deedes.

X
'Thereto she is full faire, and rich attired,
With golden hands and silver feete beside,
That many lords have her to wife desired:
But she them all despiseth for great pride.'
'Now by my life,' sayd he, 'and God to guide,
None other way will I this day betake,
But by that bridge, whereas he doth abide:
Therefore me thither lead.' No more he spake,
But thitherward forthright his ready way did make.

XI
Unto the place he came within a while,
Where on the bridge he ready armed saw
The Sarazin, awayting for some spoile.
Who as they to the passage gan to draw,
A villaine to them came with scull all raw,
That passage money did of them require,
According to the custome of their law.
To whom he aunswerd wroth, 'Loe! there thy hire;'
And with that word him strooke, that streight he did expire.

XII
Which when the Pagan saw, he wexed wroth,
And streight him selfe unto the fight addrest,
Ne was Sir Artegall behinde: so both
Together ran with ready speares in rest.
Right in the midst, whereas they brest to brest
Should meete, a trap was letten downe to fall
Into the floud: streight leapt the carle unblest,
Well weening that his foe was falne withall:
But he was well aware, and leapt before his fall.

XIII
There being both together in the floud,

They each at other tyrannously flew;
Ne ought the water cooled their whot bloud,
But rather in them kindled choler new.
But there the Paynim, who that use well knew
To fight in water, great advantage had,
That oftentimes him nigh he overthrew:
And eke the courser whereuppon he rad
Could swim like to a fish, whiles he his backe bestrad.

XIV
Which oddes when as Sir Artegall espide,
He saw no way but close with him in hast;
And to him driving strongly downe the tide,
Uppon his iron coller griped fast,
That with the straint his wesand nigh he brast.
There they together strove and struggled long,
Either the other from his steede to cast;
Ne ever Artegall his griple strong
For any thing wold slacke, but still uppon him hong.

XV
As when a dolphin and a sele are met
In the wide champian of the ocean plaine:
With cruell chaufe their courages they whet,
The maysterdome of each by force to gaine,
And dreadfull battaile twixt them do darraine:
They snuf, they snort, they bounce, they rage, they rore,
That all the sea, disturbed with their traine,
Doth frie with fome above the surges hore:
Such was betwixt these two the troublesome uprore.

XVI
So Artegall at length him forst forsake
His horses backe, for dread of being drownd,
And to his handy swimming him betake.
Eftsoones him selfe he from his hold unbownd,
And then no ods at all in him he fownd:
For Artegall in swimming skilfull was,
And durst the depth of any water sownd.
So ought each knight, that use of perill has,
In swimming be expert, through waters force to pas.

XVII
Then very doubtfull was the warres event,
Uncertaine whether had the better side:
For both were skild in that experiment,
And both in armes well traind and throughly tride.
But Artegall was better breath'd beside,
And towards th' end grew greater in his might,
That his faint foe no longer could abide
His puissance, ne beare him selfe upright,

But from the water to the land betooke his flight.

XVIII
But Artegall pursewd him still so neare,
With bright Chrysaor in his cruell hand,
That, as his head he gan a litle reare
Above the brincke, to tread upon the land,
He smote it off, that tumbling on the strand
It bit the earth for very fell despight,
And gnashed with his teeth, as if he band
High God, whose goodnesse he despaired quight,
Or curst the hand which did that vengeance on him dight.

XIX
His corps was carried downe along the lee,
Whose waters with his filthy bloud it stayned:
But his blasphemous head, that all might see,
He pitcht upon a pole on high ordayned;
Where many years it afterwards remayned,
To be a mirrour to all mighty men,
In whose right hands great power is contayned,
That none of them the feeble overren,
But alwaies doe their powre within just compasse pen.

XX
That done, unto the castle he did wend,
In which the Paynims daughter did abide,
Guarded of many which did her defend:
Of whom he entrance sought, but was denide,
And with reprochfull blasphemy defide,
Beaten with stones downe from the battilment,
That he was forced to withdraw aside;
And bad his servant Talus to invent
Which way he enter might without endangerment.

XXI
Eftsoones his page drew to the castle gate,
And with his iron flaile at it let flie,
That all the warders it did sore amate,
The which erewhile spake so reprochfully,
And made them stoupe, that looked earst so hie.
Yet still he bet and bounst uppon the dore,
And thundred strokes thereon so hideouslie,
That all the peece he shaked from the flore,
And filled all the house with feare and great uprore.

XXII
With noise whereof the lady forth appeared
Uppon the castle wall; and when she saw
The daungerous state in which she stood, she feared
The sad effect of her neare overthrow;

And gan entreat that iron man below
To cease his outrage, and him faire besought,
Sith neither force of stones which they did throw,
Nor powr of charms, which she against him wrought,
Might otherwise prevaile, or make him cease for ought.

XXIII
But when as yet she saw him to proceede,
Unmov'd with praiers or with piteous thought,
She ment him to corrupt with goodly meede;
And causde great sackes with endlesse riches fraught,
Unto the battilment to be upbrought,
And powred forth over the castle wall,
That she might win some time, though dearly bought,
Whilest he to gathering of the gold did fall.
But he was nothing mov'd nor tempted therewithall;

XXIV
But still continu'd his assault the more,
And layd on load with his huge yron flaile,
That at the length he has yrent the dore,
And made way for his maister to assaile.
Who being entred, nought did then availe
For wight, against his powre them selves to reare:
Each one did flie; their hearts began to faile;
And hid them selves in corners here and there;
And eke their dame halfe dead did hide her self for feare.

XXV
Long they her sought, yet no where could they finde her,
That sure they ween'd she was escapt away:
But Talus, that could like a limehound winde her,
And all things secrete wisely could bewray,
At length found out whereas she hidden lay
Under an heape of gold. Thence he her drew
By the faire lockes, and fowly did array,
Withouten pitty of her goodly hew,
That Artegall him selfe her seemelesse plight did rew.

XXVI
Yet for no pitty would he change the course
Of justice, which in Talus hand did lye;
Who rudely hayld her forth without remorse,
Still holding up her suppliant hands on hye,
And kneeling at his feete submissively.
But he her suppliant hands, those hands of gold,
And eke her feete, those feete of silver trye,
Which sought unrighteousnesse, and justice sold,
Chopt off, and nayld on high, that all might them behold.

XXVII

Her selfe then tooke he by the sclender wast,
In vaine loud crying, and into the flood
Over the castle wall adowne her cast,
And there her drowned in the durty mud:
But the streame washt away her guilty blood.
Thereafter all that mucky pelfe he tooke,
The spoile of peoples evill gotten good,
The which her sire had scrap't by hooke and crooke,
And burning all to ashes, powr'd it downe the brooke.

XXVIII
And lastly all that castle quite he raced,
Even from the sole of his foundation,
And all the hewen stones thereof defaced,
That there mote be no hope of reparation,
Nor memory thereof to any nation.
All which when Talus throughly had perfourmed,
Sir Artegall undid the evill fashion,
And wicked customes of that bridge refourmed:
Which done, unto his former journey he retourned.

XXIX
In which they measur'd mickle weary way,
Till that at length nigh to the sea they drew;
By which as they did travell on a day,
They saw before them, far as they could vew,
Full many people gathered in a crew;
Whose great assembly they did much admire;
For never there the like resort they knew.
So towards them they coasted, to enquire
What thing so many nations met did there desire.

XXX
There they beheld a mighty gyant stand
Upon a rocke, and holding forth on hie
An huge great paire of ballance in his hand,
With which he boasted in his surquedrie,
That all the world he would weigh equallie,
If ought he had the same to counterpoys.
For want whereof he weighed vanity,
And fild his ballaunce full of idle toys:
Yet was admired much of fooles, women, and boys.

XXXI
He sayd that he would all the earth uptake,
And all the sea, devided each from either:
So would he of the fire one ballaunce make,
And one of th' ayre, without or wind or wether:
Then would he ballaunce heaven and hell together,
And all that did within them all containe;
Of all whose weight he would not misse a fether:

And looke what surplus did of each remaine,
He would to his owne part restore the same againe.

XXXII
Forwhy, he sayd, they all unequall were,
And had encroched uppon others share,
Like as the sea (which plaine he shewed there)
Had worne the earth, so did the fire the aire,
So all the rest did others parts empaire,
And so were realmes and nations run awry.
All which he undertooke for to repaire,
In sort as they were formed aunciently;
And all things would reduce unto equality.

XXXIII
Therefore the vulgar did about him flocke,
And cluster thicke unto his leasings vaine,
Like foolish flies about an hony crocke,
In hope by him great benefite to gaine,
And uncontrolled freedome to obtaine.
All which when Artegall did see and heare,
How he mis-led the simple peoples traine,
In sdeignfull wize he drew unto him neare,
And thus unto him spake, without regard or feare:

XXXIV
'Thou that presum'st to weigh the world anew,
And all things to an equall to restore,
In stead of right me seemes great wrong dost shew,
And far above thy forces pitch to sore.
For ere thou limit what is lesse or more
In every thing, thou oughtest first to know,
What was the poyse of every part of yore:
And looke then, how much it doth overflow,
Or faile thereof, so much is more then just to trow.

XXXV
'For at the first they all created were
In goodly measure by their Makers might,
And weighed out in ballaunces so nere,
That not a dram was missing of their right:
The earth was in the middle centre pight,
In which it doth immoveable abide,
Hemd in with waters like a wall in sight;
And they with aire, that not a drop can slide:
Al which the heavens containe, and in their courses guide.

XXXVI
'Such heavenly justice doth among them raine,
That every one doe know their certaine bound,
In which they doe these many yeares remaine,

And mongst them al no change hath yet beene found.
But if thou now shouldst weigh them new in pound,
We are not sure they would so long remaine:
All change is perillous, and all chaunce unsound.
Therefore leave off to weigh them all againe,
Till we may be assur'd they shall their course retaine.'

XXXVII
'Thou foolishe Elfe,' said then the gyant wroth,
'Seest not, how badly all things present bee,
And each estate quite out of order goth?
The sea it selfe doest thou not plainely see
Encroch uppon the land there under thee;
And th' earth it selfe how daily its increast
By all that dying to it turned be?
Were it not good that wrong were then surceast,
And from the most, that some were given to the least?

XXXVIII
'Therefore I will throw downe these mountaines hie,
And make them levell with the lowly plaine:
These towring rocks, which reach unto the skie,
I will thrust downe into the deepest maine,
And as they were, them equalize againe.
Tyrants, that make men subject to their law,
I will suppresse, that they no more may raine;
And lordings curbe, that commons over-aw;
And all the wealth of rich men to the poore will draw.'

XXXIX
'Of things unseene how canst thou deeme aright,'
Then answered the righteous Artegall,
'Sith thou misdeem'st so much of things in sight?
What though the sea with waves continuall
Doe eate the earth? it is no more at all,
Ne is the earth the lesse, or loseth ought:
For whatsoever from one place doth fall
Is with the tide unto an other brought:
For there is nothing lost, that may be found, if sought.

XL
'Likewise the earth is not augmented more
By all that dying into it doe fade:
For of the earth they formed were of yore;
How ever gay their blossome or their blade
Doe flourish now, they into dust shall vade.
What wrong then is it, if that when they die,
They turne to that whereof they first were made?
All in the powre of their great Maker lie:
All creatures must obey the voice of the Most Hie.

XLI

'They live, they die, like as He doth ordaine,
Ne ever any asketh reason why.
The hils doe not the lowly dales disdaine;
The dales doe not the lofty hils envy.
He maketh kings to sit in soverainty;
He maketh subjects to their power obay;
He pulleth downe, He setteth up on by;
He gives to this, from that He takes away:
For all we have is His: what He list doe, He may.

XLII

'What ever thing is done, by Him is donne,
Ne any may His mighty will withstand;
Ne any may His soveraine power shonne,
Ne loose that He hath bound with stedfast band.
In vaine therefore doest thou now take in hand,
To call to count, or weigh His workes anew,
Whose counsels depth thou canst not understand;
Sith of things subject to thy daily vew
Thou doest not know the causes, nor their courses dew.

XLIII

'For take thy ballaunce, if thou be so wise,
And weigh the winde that under heaven doth blow;
Or weigh the light that in the East doth rise;
Or weigh the thought that from mans mind doth flow.
But if the weight of these thou canst not show,
Weigh but one word which from thy lips doth fall:
For how canst thou those greater secrets know,
That doest not know the least thing of them all?
Ill can he rule the great, that cannot reach the small.'

XLIV

Therewith the gyant much abashed sayd,
That he of little things made reckoning light,
Yet the least word that ever could be layd
Within his ballaunce he could way aright.
'Which is,' sayd he, 'more heavy then in weight,
The right or wrong, the false or else the trew?'
He answered that he would try it streight:
So he the words into his ballaunce threw;
But streight the winged words out of his ballaunce flew.

XLV

Wroth wext he then, and sayd that words were light,
Ne would within his ballaunce well abide:
But he could justly weigh the wrong or right.
'Well then,' sayd Artegall, 'let it be tride.
First in one ballance set the true aside.'
He did so first; and then the false he layd

In th' other scale; but still it downe did slide,
And by no meane could in the weight be stayd:
For by no meanes the false will with the truth be wayd.

XLVI
'Now take the right likewise,' sayd Artegale,
'And counterpeise the same with so much wrong.'
So first the right he put into one scale;
And then the gyant strove with puissance strong
To fill the other scale with so much wrong.
But all the wrongs that he therein could lay
Might not it peise; yet did he labour long,
And swat, and chauf'd, and proved every way:
Yet all the wrongs could not a litle right downe way.

XLVII
Which when he saw, he greatly grew in rage,
And almost would his balances have broken:
But Artegall him fairely gan asswage,
And said: 'Be not upon thy balance wroken;
For they doe nought but right or wrong betoken;
But in the mind the doome of right must bee:
And so likewise of words, the which be spoken,
The eare must be the ballance, to decree
And judge, whether with truth or falshood they agree.

XLVIII
'But set the truth and set the right aside,
For they with wrong or falshood will not fare;
And put two wrongs together to be tride,
Or else two falses, of each equall share,
And then together doe them both compare:
For truth is one, and right is ever one.'
So did he, and then plaine it did appeare,
Whether of them the greater were attone.
But right sate in the middest of the beame alone.

XLIX
But he the right from thence did thrust away,
For it was not the right which he did seeke;
But rather strove extremities to way,
Th' one to diminish, th' other for to eeke:
For of the meane he greatly did misleeke.
Whom when so lewdly minded Talus found,
Approching nigh unto him, cheeke by cheeke,
He shouldered him from off the higher ground,
And down the rock him throwing, in the sea him dround.

L
Like as a ship, whom cruell tempest drives
Upon a rocke with horrible dismay,

Her shattered ribs in thousand peeces rives,
And spoyling all her geares and goodly ray,
Does make her selfe misfortunes piteous pray:
So downe the cliffe the wretched gyant tumbled;
His battred ballances in peeces lay,
His timbered bones all broken rudely rumbled:
So was the high aspyring with huge ruine humbled.

LI
That when the people, which had there about
Long wayted, saw his sudden desolation,
They gan to gather in tumultuous rout,
And mutining, to stirre up civill faction,
For certaine losse of so great expectation.
For well they hoped to have got great good,
And wondrous riches by his innovation.
Therefore resolving to revenge his blood,
They rose in armes, and all in battell order stood.

LII
Which lawlesse multitude him comming too,
In warlike wise, when Artegall did vew,
He much was troubled, ne wist what to doo.
For loth he was his noble hands t' embrew
In the base blood of such a rascall crew;
And otherwise, if that he should retire,
He fear'd least they with shame would him pursew.
Therefore he Talus to them sent, t' inquire
The cause of their array, and truce for to desire.

LIII
But soone as they him nigh approching spide,
They gan with all their weapons him assay,
And rudely stroke at him on every side:
Yet nought they could him hurt, ne ought dismay.
But when at them he with his flaile gan lay,
He like a swarme of flyes them overthrew;
Ne any of them durst come in his way,
But here and there before his presence flew,
And hid themselves in holes and bushes from his vew.

LIV
As when a faulcon hath with nimble flight
Flowne at a flush of ducks, foreby the brooke,
The trembling foule, dismayd with dreadfull sight
Of death, the which them almost overtooke,
Doe hide themselves from her astonying looke
Amongst the flags and covert round about.
When Talus saw they all the field for-sooke,
And none appear'd of all that raskall rout,
To Artegall he turn'd, and went with him throughout.

CANTO III

The spousals of faire Florimell,
Where turney many knights:
There Braggadochio is uncas'd
In all the ladies sights.

I
After long stormes and tempests overblowne,
The sunne at length his joyous face doth cleare:
So when as Fortune all her spight hath showne,
Some blisfull houres at last must needes appeare;
Else should afflicted wights oftimes despeire.
So comes it now to Florimell by tourne,
After long sorrowes suffered whyleare,
In which captiv'd she many moneths did mourne,
To tast of joy, and to wont pleasures to retourne.

II
Who being freed from Proteus cruell band
By Marinell, was unto him affide,
And by him brought againe to Faerie Land;
Where he her spous'd, and made his joyous bride.
The time and place was blazed farre and wide,
And solemne feasts and giusts ordain'd therefore.
To which there did resort from every side
Of lords and ladies infinite great store;
Ne any knight was absent, that brave courage bore.

III
To tell the glorie of the feast that day,
The goodly service, the devicefull sights,
The bridegromes state, the brides most rich aray,
The pride of ladies, and the worth of knights,
The royall banquets, and the rare delights
Were worke fit for an herauld, not for me:
But for so much as to my lot here lights,
That with this present treatise doth agree,
True vertue to advance, shall here recounted bee.

IV
When all men had with full satietie
Of meates and drinkes their appetites suffiz'd,
To deedes of armes and proofe of chevalrie
They gan themselves addresse, full rich aguiz'd,
As each one had his furnitures deviz'd.

And first of all issu'd Sir Marinell,
And with him sixe knights more, which enterpriz'd
To chalenge all in right of Florimell,
And to maintaine that she all others did excell.

V
The first of them was hight Sir Orimont,
A noble knight, and tride in hard assayes;
The second had to name Sir Bellisont,
But second unto none in prowesse prayse;
The third was Brunell, famous in his dayes;
The fourth Ecastor, of exceeding might;
The fift Armeddan, skild in lovely layes;
The sixt was Lansack, a redoubted knight:
All sixe well seene in armes, and prov'd in many a fight.

VI
And them against came all that list to giust,
From every coast and countrie under sunne:
None was debard, but all had leave that lust.
The trompets sound; then all together ronne.
Full many deedes of armes that day were donne,
And many knights unhorst, and many wounded,
As fortune fell; yet litle lost or wonne:
But all that day the greatest prayse redounded
To Marinell, whose name the heralds loud resounded.

VII
The second day, so soone as morrow light
Appear'd in heaven, into the field they came,
And there all day continew'd cruell fight,
With divers fortune fit for such a game,
In which all strove with perill to winne fame.
Yet whether side was victor note be ghest:
But at the last the trompets did proclame
That Marinell that day deserved best.
So they disparted were, and all men went to rest.

VIII
The third day came, that should due tryall lend
Of all the rest, and then this warlike crew
Together met, of all to make an end.
There Marinell great deeds of armes did shew;
And through the thickest like a lyon flew,
Rashing off helmes, and ryving plates a sonder,
That every one his daunger did eschew.
So terribly his dreadfull strokes did thonder,
That all men stood amaz'd, and at his might did wonder.

IX
But what on earth can alwayes happie stand?

The greater prowesse greater perils find.
So farre he past amongst his enemies band,
That they have him enclosed so behind,
As by no meanes he can himselfe outwind.
And now perforce they have him prisoner taken;
And now they doe with captive bands him bind;
And now they lead him thence, of all forsaken,
Unlesse some succour had in time him overtaken.

X
It fortun'd whylest they were thus ill beset,
Sir Artegall into the tilt-yard came,
With Braggadochio, whom he lately met
Upon the way, with that his snowy dame.
Where when he understood by common fame
What evill hap to Marinell betid,
He much was mov'd at so unworthie shame,
And streight that boaster prayd, with whom he rid,
To change his shield with him, to be the better hid.

XI
So forth he went, and soone them over hent,
Where they were leading Marinell away;
Whom he assayld with dreadlesse hardiment,
And forst the burden of their prize to stay.
They were an hundred knights of that array;
Of which th' one halfe upon himselfe did set,
The other stayd behind to gard the pray.
But he ere long the former fiftie bet;
And from the other fiftie soone the prisoner fet.

XII
So backe he brought Sir Marinell againe;
Whom having quickly arm'd againe anew,
They both together joyned might and maine,
To set afresh on all the other crew.
Whom with sore havocke soone they overthrew,
And chaced quite out of the field, that none
Against them durst his head to perill shew.
So were they left lords of the field alone:
So Marinell by him was rescu'd from his fone.

XIII
Which when he had perform'd, then backe againe
To Braggadochio did his shield restore:
Who all this while behind him did remaine,
Keeping there close with him in pretious store
That his false ladie, as ye heard afore.
Then did the trompets sound, and judges rose,
And all these knights, which that day armour bore,
Came to the open hall, to listen whose

The honour of the prize should be adjudg'd by those.

XIV
And thether also came in open sight
Fayre Florimell, into the common hall,
To greet his guerdon unto every knight,
And best to him to whom the best should fall.
Then for that stranger knight they loud did call,
To whom that day they should the girlond yield:
Who came not forth: but for Sir Artegall
Came Braggadochio, and did shew his shield,
Which bore the sunne brode blazed in a golden field.

XV
The sight whereof did all with gladnesse fill:
So unto him they did addeeme the prise
Of all that tryumph. Then the trompets shrill
Don Braggadochios name resounded thrise:
So courage lent a cloke to cowardise.
And then to him came fayrest Florimell,
And goodly gan to greet his brave emprise,
And thousand thankes him yeeld, that had so well
Approv'd that day that she all others did excell.

XVI
To whom the boaster, that all knights did blot,
With proud disdaine did scornefull answere make,
That what he did that day, he did it not
For her, but for his owne deare ladies sake,
Whom on his perill he did undertake,
Both her and eke all others to excell:
And further did uncomely speaches crake.
Much did his words the gentle ladie quell,
And turn'd aside for shame to heare what he did tell.

XVII
Then forth he brought his snowy Florimele,
Whom Trompart had in keeping there beside,
Covered from peoples gazement with a vele.
Whom when discovered they had throughly eide,
With great amazement they were stupefide;
And said, that surely Florimell it was,
Or if it were not Florimell so tride,
That Florimell her selfe she then did pas.
So feeble skill of perfect things the vulgar has.

XVIII
Which when as Marinell beheld likewise,
He was therewith exceedingly dismayd;
Ne wist he what to thinke, or to devise,
But, like as one whom feends had made affrayd,

He long astonisht stood, ne ought he sayd,
Ne ought he did, but with fast fixed eies
He gazed still upon that snowy mayd;
Whom ever as he did the more avize,
The more to be true Florimell he did surmize.

XIX
As when two sunnes appeare in the azure skye,
Mounted in Phœbus charet fierie bright,
Both darting forth faire beames to each mans eye,
And both adorn'd with lampes of flaming light,
All that behold so strange prodigious sight,
Not knowing Natures worke, nor what to weene,
Are rapt with wonder and with rare affright:
So stood Sir Marinell, when he had seene
The semblant of this false by his faire beauties queene.

XX
All which when Artegall, who all this while
Stood in the preasse close covered, well advewed,
And saw that boasters pride and gracelesse guile,
He could no longer beare, but forth issewed,
And unto all himselfe there open shewed,
And to the boaster said: 'Thou losell base,
That hast with borrowed plumes thy selfe endewed,
And others worth with leasings doest deface,
When they are all restor'd, thou shalt rest in disgrace.

XXI
'That shield, which thou doest beare, was it indeed,
Which this dayes honour sav'd to Marinell;
But not that arme, nor thou the man, I reed,
Which didst that service unto Florimell.
For proofe shew forth thy sword, and let it tell
What strokes, what dreadfull stoure it stird this day:
Or shew the wounds which unto thee befell;
Or shew the sweat with which thou diddest sway
So sharpe a battell, that so many did dismay.

XXII
'But this the sword which wrought those cruell stounds,
And this the arme the which that shield did beare,
And these the signes,' (so shewed forth his wounds)
'By which that glorie gotten doth appeare.
As for this ladie, which he sheweth here,
Is not (I wager) Florimell at all;
But some fayre franion, fit for such a fere,
That by misfortune in his hand did fall.'
For proofe whereof, he bad them Florimell forth call.

XXIII

So forth the noble ladie was ybrought,
Adorn'd with honor and all comely grace:
Whereto her bashfull shamefastnesse ywrought
A great increase in her faire blushing face;
As roses did with lillies interlace.
For of those words, the which that boaster threw,
She inly yet conceived great disgrace.
Whom when as all the people such did vew,
They shouted loud, and signes of gladnesse all did shew.

XXIV
Then did he set her by that snowy one,
Like the true saint beside the image set,
Of both their beauties to make paragone,
And triall, whether should the honor get.
Streight way so soone as both together met,
Th' enchaunted damzell vanisht into nought:
Her snowy substance melted as with heat,
Ne of that goodly hew remayned ought,
But th' emptie girdle, which about her wast was wrought.

XXV
As when the daughter of Thaumantes faire
Hath in a watry cloud displayed wide
Her goodly bow, which paints the liquid ayre;
That all men wonder at her colours pride;
All suddenly, ere one can looke aside,
The glorious picture vanisheth away,
Ne any token doth thereof abide:
So did this ladies goodly forme decay,
And into nothing goe, ere one could it bewray.

XXVI
Which when as all that present were beheld,
They stricken were with great astonishment,
And their faint harts with senselesse horrour queld,
To see the thing, that seem'd so excellent,
So stolen from their fancies wonderment;
That what of it became none understood.
And Braggadochio selfe with dreriment
So daunted was, in his despeyring mood,
That like a lifelesse corse immoveable he stood.

XXVII
But Artegall that golden belt uptooke,
The which of all her spoyle was onely left;
Which was not hers, as many it mistooke,
But Florimells owne girdle, from her reft,
While she was flying, like a weary weft,
From that foule monster which did her compell
To perils great; which he unbuckling eft,

Presented to the fayrest Florimell;
Who round about her tender wast it fitted well.

XXVIII
Full many ladies often had assayd
About their middles that faire belt to knit;
And many a one suppos'd to be a mayd:
Yet it to none of all their loynes would fit,
Till Florimell about her fastned it.
Such power it had, that to no womans wast
By any skill or labour it would sit,
Unlesse that she were continent and chast,
But it would lose or breake, that many had disgrast.

XXIX
Whilest thus they busied were bout Florimell,
And boastfull Braggadochio to defame,
Sir Guyon, as by fortune then befell,
Forth from the thickest preasse of people came,
His owne good steed, which he had stolne, to clame;
And th' one hand seizing on his golden bit,
With th' other drew his sword: for with the same
He ment the thiefe there deadly to have smit:
And had he not bene held, he nought had fayld of it.

XXX
Thereof great hurly burly moved was
Throughout the hall, for that same warlike horse:
For Braggadochio would not let him pas;
And Guyon would him algates have perforse,
Or it approve upon his carrion corse.
Which troublous stirre when Artegall perceived,
He nigh them drew to stay th' avengers forse,
And gan inquire how was that steed bereaved,
Whether by might extort, or else by slight deceaved.

XXXI
Who all that piteous storie, which befell
About that wofull couple which were slaine,
And their young bloodie babe, to him gantell;
With whom whiles he did in the wood remaine,
His horse purloyned was by subtill traine:
For which he chalenged the thiefe to fight.
But he for nought could him thereto constraine;
For as the death he hated such despight,
And rather had to lose, then trie in armes his right.

XXXII
Which Artegall well hearing, though no more
By law of armes there neede ones right to trie,
As was the wont of warlike knights of yore,

Then that his foe should him the field denie,
Yet further right by tokens to descrie,
He askt what privie tokens he did beare.
'If that,' said Guyon, 'may you satisfie,
Within his mouth a blacke spot doth appeare,
Shapt like a horses shoe, who list to seeke it there.'

XXXIII
Whereof to make due tryall, one did take
The horse in hand, within his mouth to looke:
But with his heeles so sorely he him strake,
That all his ribs he quite in peeces broke,
That never word from that day forth he spoke.
Another, that would seeme to have more wit,
Him by the bright embrodered hedstall tooke:
But by the shoulder him so sore he bit,
That he him maymed quite, and all his shoulder split.

XXXIV
Ne he his mouth would open unto wight,
Untill that Guyon selfe unto him spake,
And called Brigadore (so was he hight);
Whose voice so soone as he did undertake,
Eftsoones he stood as still as any stake,
And suffred all his secret marke to see:
And when as he him nam'd, for joy he brake
His bands, and follow'd him with gladfull glee,
And friskt, and flong aloft, and louted low on knee.

XXXV
Thereby Sir Artegall did plaine areed,
That unto him the horse belong'd, and sayd:
'Lo there, Sir Guyon, take to you the steed,
As he with golden saddle is arayd;
And let that losell, plainely now displayd,
Hence fare on foot, till he an horse have gayned.'
But the proud boaster gan his doome upbrayd,
And him revil'd, and rated, and disdayned,
That judgement so unjust against him had ordayned.

XXXVI
Much was the knight incenst with his lewd word,
To have revenged that his villeny;
And thrise did lay his hand upon his sword,
To have him slaine, or dearely doen aby.
But Guyon did his choler pacify,
Saying, 'Sir knight, it would dishonour bee
To you, that are our judge of equity,
To wreake your wrath on such a carle as hee:
It 's punishment enough, that all his shame doe see.'

XXXVII

So did he mitigate Sir Artegall;
But Talus by the backe the boaster hent,
And drawing him out of the open hall,
Upon him did inflict this punishment:
First he his beard did shave, and fowly shent;
Then from him reft his shield, and it renverst,
And blotted out his armes with falshood blent,
And himselfe baffuld, and his armes unherst,
And broke his sword in twaine, and all his armour sperst.

XXXVIII

The whiles his guilefull groome was fled away:
But vaine it was to thinke from him to flie.
Who overtaking him did disaray,
And all his face deform'd with infamie,
And out of court him scourged openly.
So ought all faytours, that true knighthood shame,
And armes dishonour with base villanie,
From all brave knights be banisht with defame:
For oft their lewdnes blotteth good deserts with blame.

XXXIX

Now when these counterfeits were thus uncased
Out of the foreside of their forgerie,
And in the sight of all men cleane disgraced,
All gan to jest and gibe full merilie
At the remembrance of their knaverie.
Ladies can laugh at ladies, knights at knights,
To thinke with how great vaunt of braverie
He them abused, through his subtill slights,
And what a glorious shew he made in all their sights.

XL

There leave we them in pleasure and repast
Spending their joyous dayes and gladfull nights,
And taking usurie of time forepast,
With all deare delices and rare delights,
Fit for such ladies and such lovely knights:
And turne we here to this faire furrowes end
Our wearie yokes, to gather fresher sprights,
That, when as time to Artegall shall tend,
We on his first adventure may him forward send.

CANTO IV

Artegall dealeth right betwixt
Two brethren that doe strive;

Saves Terpine from the gallow tree,
And doth from death reprive.

I
Who so upon him selfe will take the skill
True justice unto people to divide,
Had neede have mightie hands, for to fulfill
That which he doth with righteous doome decide,
And for to maister wrong and puissant pride.
For vaine it is to deeme of things aright,
And makes wrong doers justice to deride,
Unlesse it be perform'd with dreadlesse might:
For powre is the right hand of Justice truely hight.

II
Therefore whylome to knights of great emprise
The charge of Justice given was in trust,
That they might execute her judgements wise,
And with their might beat downe licentious lust,
Which proudly did impugne her sentence just.
Whereof no braver president this day
Remaines on earth, preserv'd from yron rust
Of rude oblivion, and long times decay,
Then this of Artegall, which here we have to say.

III
Who, having lately left that lovely payre,
Enlincked fast in wedlockes loyall bond,
Bold Marinell with Florimell the fayre,
With whom great feast and goodly glee he fond,
Departed from the Castle of the Strond,
To follow his adventures first intent,
Which long agoe he taken had in hond:
Ne wight with him for his assistance went,
But that great yron groome, his gard and government.

IV
With whom as he did passe by the sea shore,
He chaunst to come whereas two comely squires,
Both brethren, whom one wombe together bore,
But stirred up with different desires,
Together strove, and kindled wrathfull fires:
And them beside two seemely damzels stood,
By all meanes seeking to asswage their ires,
Now with faire words; but words did little good,
Now with sharpe threats; but threats the more increast their mood.

V
And there before them stood a coffer strong,
Fast bound on every side with iron bands,

But seeming to have suffred mickle wrong,
Either by being wreckt uppon the sands,
Or being carried farre from forraine lands.
Seem'd that for it these squires at ods did fall,
And bent against them selves their cruell hands.
But evermore, those damzels did forestall
Their furious encounter, and their fiercenesse pall.

VI
But firmely fixt they were, with dint of sword
And battailes doubtfull proofe their rights to try,
Ne other end their fury would afford,
But what to them fortune would justify.
So stood they both in readinesse, thereby
To joyne the combate with cruell intent;
When Artegall arriving happily,
Did stay a while their greedy bickerment,
Till he had questioned the cause of their dissent.

VII
To whom the elder did this aunswere frame:
'Then weete ye, sir, that we two brethren be,
To whom our sire, Milesio by name,
Did equally bequeath his lands in fee,
Two ilands, which ye there before you see
Not farre in sea; of which the one appeares
But like a little mount of small degree;
Yet was as great and wide ere many yeares,
As that same other isle, that greater bredth now beares.

VIII
'But tract of time, that all things doth decay,
And this devouring sea, that naught doth spare,
The most part of my land hath washt away,
And throwne it up unto my brothers share:
So his encreased, but mine did empaire.
Before which time I lov'd, as was my lot,
That further mayd, hight Philtera the faire,
With whom a goodly doure I should have got,
And should have joyned bene to her in wedlocks knot.

IX
'Then did my younger brother Amidas
Love that same other damzell, Lucy bright,
To whom but little dowre allotted was;
Her vertue was the dowre that did delight.
What better dowre can to a dame be hight?
But now when Philtra saw my lands decay,
And former livelod fayle, she left me quight,
And to my brother did ellope streight way:
Who, taking her from me, his owne love left astray.

X
'She seeing then her selfe forsaken so,
Through dolorous despaire, which she conceyved,
Into the sea her selfe did headlong throw,
Thinking to have her griefe by death bereaved.
But see how much her purpose was deceaved.
Whilest thus amidst the billowes beating of her
Twixt life and death, long to and fro she weaved,
She chaunst unwares to light uppon this coffer,
Which to her in that daunger hope of life did offer.

XI
'The wretched mayd, that earst desir'd to die,
When as the paine of death she tasted had,
And but halfe seene his ugly visnomie,
Gan to repent that she had beene so mad,
For any death to chaunge life, though most bad:
And catching hold of this sea-beaten chest,
The lucky pylot of her passage sad,
After long tossing in the seas distrest,
Her weary barke at last uppon mine isle did rest.

XII
'Where I, by chaunce then wandring on the shore,
Did her espy, and through my good endevour
From dreadfull mouth of death, which threatned sore
Her to have swallow'd up, did helpe to save her.
She then, in recompence of that great favour
Which I on her bestowed, bestowed on me
The portion of that good which fortune gave her,
Together with her selfe in dowry free;
Both goodly portions, but of both the better she.

XIII
'Yet in this coffer, which she with her brought,
Great threasure sithence we did finde contained;
Which as our owne we tooke, and so it thought.
But this same other damzell since hath fained,
That to her selfe that threasure appertained;
And that she did transport the same by sea,
To bring it to her husband new ordained,
But suffred cruell shipwracke by the way.
But whether it be so or no, I can not say.

XIV
'But whether it indeede be so or no,
This doe I say, that what so good or ill
Or God or Fortune unto me did throw,
Not wronging any other by my will,
I hold mine owne, and so will hold it still.

And though my land he first did winne away,
And then my love (though now it little skill)
Yet my good lucke he shall not likewise pray;
But I will it defend, whilst ever that I may.'

XV
So having sayd, the younger did ensew:
'Full true it is, what so about our land
My brother here declared hath to you:
But not for it this ods twixt us doth stand,
But for this threasure throwne uppon his strand;
Which well I prove, as shall appeare by triall,
To be this maides with whom I fastned hand,
Known by good markes and perfect good espiall,
Therefore it ought be rendred her without deniall.'

XVI
When they thus ended had, the knight began:
'Certes your strife were easie to accord,
Would ye remit it to some righteous man.'
'Unto your selfe,' said they, 'we give our word,
To bide what judgement ye shall us afford.'
'Then for assuraunce to my doome to stand,
Under my foote let each lay downe his sword,
And then you shall my sentence understand.'
So each of them layd downe his sword out of his hand.

XVII
Then Artegall thus to the younger sayd:
'Now tell me, Amidas, if that ye may,
Your brothers land, the which the sea hath layd
Unto your part, and pluckt from his away,
By what good right doe you withhold this day?'
'What other right,' quoth he, 'should you esteeme,
But that the sea it to my share did lay?'
'Your right is good,' sayd he, 'and so I deeme,
That what the sea unto you sent your own should seeme.'

XVIII
Then turning to the elder thus he sayd:
'Now, Bracidas, let this likewise be showne:
Your brothers threasure, which from him is strayd,
Being the dowry of his wife well knowne,
By what right doe you claime to be your owne?'
'What other right,' quoth he, 'should you esteeme,
But that the sea hath it unto me throwne?'
'Your right is good,' sayd he, 'and so I deeme,
That what the sea unto you sent your own should seeme.

XIX
'For equall right in equall things doth stand;

For what the mighty sea hath once possest,
And plucked quite from all possessors hand,
Whether by rage of waves, that never rest,
Or else by wracke, that wretches hath distrest,
He may dispose by his imperiall might,
As thing at randon left, to whom he list.
So, Amidas, the land was yours first hight,
And so the threasure yours is, Bracidas, by right.'

XX
When he his sentence thus pronounced had,
Both Amidas and Philtra were displeased:
But Bracidas and Lucy were right glad,
And on the threasure by that judgement seased.
So was their discord by this doome appeased,
And each one had his right. Then Artegall,
When as their sharpe contention he had ceased,
Departed on his way, as did befall,
To follow his old quest, the which him forth did call.

XXI
So as he travelled uppon the way,
He chaunst to come, where happily he spide
A rout of many people farre away;
To whom his course he hastily applide,
To weete the cause of their assemblaunce wide.
To whom when he approched neare in sight,
(An uncouth sight) he plainely then descride
To be a troupe of women warlike dight,
With weapons in their hands, as ready for to fight.

XXII
And in the midst of them he saw a knight,
With both his hands behinde him pinnoed hard,
And round about his necke an halter tight,
As ready for the gallow tree prepard:
His face was covered, and his head was bar'd,
That who he was uneath was to descry;
And with full heavy heart with them he far'd,
Griev'd to the soule, and groning inwardly,
That he of womens hands so base a death should dy.

XXIII
But they like tyrants, mercilesse the more,
Rejoyced at his miserable case,
And him reviled, and reproched sore
With bitter taunts, and termes of vile disgrace.
Now when as Artegall, arriv'd in place,
Did aske what cause brought that man to decay,
They round about him gan to swarme apace,
Meaning on him their cruell hands to lay,

And to have wrought unwares some villanous assay.

XXIV
But he was soone aware of their ill minde,
And drawing backe deceived their intent;
Yet though him selfe did shame on womankinde
His mighty hand to shend, he Talus sent
To wrecke on them their follies hardyment:
Who with few sowces of his yron flale
Dispersed all their troupe incontinent,
And sent them home to tell a piteous tale
Of their vaine prowesse turned to their proper bale.

XXV
But that same wretched man, ordaynd to die,
They left behind them, glad to be so quit:
Him Talus tooke out of perplexitie,
And horrour of fowle death for knight unfit,
Who more then losse of life ydreaded it;
And him restoring unto living light,
So brought unto his lord, where he did sit,
Beholding all that womanish weake fight;
Whom soone as he beheld, he knew, and thus behight:

XXVI
'Sir Turpine, haplesse man, what make you here?
Or have you lost your selfe and your discretion,
That ever in this wretched case ye were?
Or have ye yeelded you to proude oppression
Of womens powre, that boast of mens subjection?
Or else what other deadly dismall day
Is falne on you, by heavens hard direction,
That ye were runne so fondly far astray,
As for to lead your selfe unto your owne decay?'

XXVII
Much was the man confounded in his mind,
Partly with shame, and partly with dismay,
That all astonisht he him selfe did find,
And little had for his excuse to say,
But onely thus: 'Most haplesse well ye may
Me justly terme, that to this shame am brought,
And made the scorne of knighthod this same day.
But who can scape what his owne fate hath wrought?
The worke of heavens will surpasseth humaine thought.'

XXVIII
'Right true: but faulty men use oftentimes
To attribute their folly unto fate,
And lay on heaven the guilt of their owne crimes.
But tell, Sir Terpin, ne let you amate

Your misery, how fell ye in this state?'
'Then sith ye needs,' quoth he, 'will know my shame,
And all the ill which chaunst to me of late,
I shortly will to you rehearse the same,
In hope ye will not turne misfortune to my blame.

XXIX
'Being desirous (as all knights are woont)
Through hard adventures deedes of armes to try,
And after fame and honour for to hunt,
I heard report that farre abrode did fly,
That a proud Amazon did late defy
All the brave knights that hold of Maidenhead,
And unto them wrought all the villany
That she could forge in her malicious head,
Which some hath put to shame, and many done be dead.

XXX
'The cause, they say, of this her cruell hate,
Is for the sake of Bellodant the bold,
To whom she bore most fervent love of late,
And wooed him by all the waies she could:
But when she saw at last, that he ne would
For ought or nought be wonne unto her will,
She turn'd her love to hatred manifold,
And for his sake vow'd to doe all the ill
Which she could doe to knights; which now she doth fulfill.

XXXI
'For all those knights, the which by force or guile
She doth subdue, she fowly doth entreate.
First she doth them of warlike armes despoile,
And cloth in womens weedes: and then with threat
Doth them compell to worke, to earne their meat,
To spin, to card, to sew, to wash, to wring;
Ne doth she give them other thing to eat,
But bread and water, or like feeble thing,
Them to disable from revenge adventuring.

XXXII
'But if through stout disdaine of manly mind,
Any her proud observaunce will withstand,
Uppon that gibbet, which is there behind,
She causeth them be hang'd up out of hand;
In which condition I right now did stand.
For being overcome by her in fight,
And put to that base service of her band,
I rather chose to die in lives despight,
Then lead that shamefull life, unworthy of a knight.'

XXXIII

'How hight that Amazon,' sayd Artegall,
'And where and how far hence does she abide?'
'Her name,' quoth he, 'they Radigund doe call,
A Princesse of great powre and greater pride,
And queene of Amazons, in armes well tride
And sundry battels, which she hath atchieved
With great successe, that her hath glorifide,
And made her famous, more then is believed;
Ne would I it have ween'd, had I not late it prieved.'

XXXIV
'Now sure,' said he, 'and by the faith that I
To Maydenhead and noble knighthood owe,
I will not rest, till I her might doe trie,
And venge the shame that she to knights doth show.
Therefore, Sir Terpin, from you lightly throw
This squalid weede, the patterne of dispaire,
And wend with me, that ye may see and know,
How fortune will your ruin'd name repaire,
And knights of Maidenhead, whose praise she would empaire.'

XXXV
With that, like one that hopelesse was repryv'd
From deathes dore, at which he lately lay,
Those yron fetters wherewith he was gyv'd,
The badges of reproch, he threw away,
And nimbly did him dight to guide the way
Unto the dwelling of that Amazone,
Which was from thence not past a mile or tway:
A goodly city and a mighty one,
The which of her owne name she called Radegone.

XXXVI
Where they arriving, by the watchman were
Described streight, who all the citty warned,
How that three warlike persons did appeare,
Of which the one him seem'd a knight all armed,
And th' other two well likely to have harmed.
Eftsoones the people all to harnesse ran,
And like a sort of bees in clusters swarmed:
Ere long their queene her selfe, halfe like a man,
Came forth into the rout, and them t' array began.

XXXVII
And now the knights, being arrived neare,
Did beat uppon the gates to enter in,
And at the porter, skorning them so few,
Threw many threats, if they the towne did win,
To teare his flesh in peeces for his sin.
Which when as Radigund there comming heard,
Her heart for rage did grate, and teeth did grin:

She bad that streight the gates should be unbard,
And to them way to make, with weapons well prepard.

XXXVIII
Soone as the gates were open to them set,
They pressed forward, entraunce to have made.
But in the middle way they were ymet
With a sharpe showre of arrowes, which them staid,
And better bad advise, ere they assaid
Unknowen perill of bold womens pride.
Then all that rout uppon them rudely laid,
And heaped strokes so fast on every side,
And arrowes haild so thicke, that they could not abide.

XXXIX
But Radigund her selfe, when she espide
Sir Terpin, from her direfull doome acquit,
So cruell doale amongst her maides divide,
T' avenge that shame they did on him commit,
All sodainely enflam'd with furious fit,
Like a fell lionesse at him she flew,
And on his head-peece him so fiercely smit,
That to the ground him quite she overthrew,
Dismayd so with the stroke that he no colours knew.

XL
Soone as she saw him on the ground to grovell,
She lightly to him leapt, and in his necke
Her proud foote setting, at his head did levell,
Weening at once her wrath on him to wreake,
And his contempt, that did her judg'ment breake.
As when a beare hath seiz'd her cruell clawes
Uppon the carkasse of some beast too weake,
Proudly stands over, and a while doth pause,
To heare the piteous beast pleading her plaintiffe cause.

XLI
Whom when as Artegall in that distresse
By chaunce beheld, he left the bloudy slaughter
In which he swam, and ranne to his redresse.
There her assayling fiercely fresh, he raught her
Such an huge stroke, that it of sence distraught her:
And had she not it warded warily,
It had depriv'd her mother of a daughter.
Nathlesse for all the powre she did apply,
It made her stagger oft, and stare with ghastly eye.

XLII
Like to an eagle in his kingly pride,
Soring through his wide empire of the aire,
To weather his brode sailes, by chaunce hath spide

A goshauke, which hath seized for her share
Uppon some fowle, that should her feast prepare;
With dreadfull force he flies at her bylive,
That with his souce, which none enduren dare,
Her from the quarrey he away doth drive,
And from her griping pounce the greedy prey doth rive.

XLIII
But soone as she her sence recover'd had,
She fiercely towards him her selfe gan dight,
Through vengeful wrath and sdeignfull pride half mad:
For never had she suffred such despight.
But ere she could joyne hand with him to fight,
Her warlike maides about her flockt so fast,
That they disparted them, maugre their might,
And with their troupes did far a sunder cast:
But mongst the rest the fight did untill evening last.

XLIV
And every while that mighty yron man,
With his strange weapon, never wont in warre,
Them sorely vext, and courst, and overran,
And broke their bowes, and did their shooting marre,
That none of all the many once did darre
Him to assault, nor once approach him nie,
But like a sort of sheepe dispersed farre
For dread of their devouring enemie,
Through all the fields and vallies did before him flie.

XLV
But when as daies faire shinie-beame, yclowded
With fearefull shadowes of deformed night,
Warn'd man and beast in quiet rest be shrowded,
Bold Radigund, with sound of trumpe on hight,
Causd all her people to surcease from fight,
And gathering them unto her citties gate,
Made them all enter in before her sight,
And all the wounded, and the weake in state,
To be convayed in, ere she would once retrate.

XLVI
When thus the field was voided all away,
And all things quieted, the Elfin knight,
Weary of toile and travell of that day,
Causd his pavilion to be richly pight
Before the city gate, in open sight;
Where he him selfe did rest in safety,
Together with Sir Terpin, all that night:
But Talus usde in times of jeopardy
To keepe a nightly watch, for dread of treachery.

XLVII
But Radigund full of heart-gnawing griefe,
For the rebuke which she sustain'd that day,
Could take no rest, ne would receive reliefe,
But tossed in her troublous minde, what way
She mote revenge that blot which on her lay.
There she resolv'd her selfe in single fight
To try her fortune, and his force assay,
Rather then see her people spoiled quight,
As she had seene that day, a disaventerous sight.

XLVIII
She called forth to her a trusty mayd,
Whom she thought fittest for that businesse,
(Her name was Clarin,) and thus to her sayd:
'Goe, damzell, quickly, doe thy selfe addresse,
To doe the message which I shall expresse
Goe thou unto that stranger Faery knight,
Who yeester day drove us to such distresse;
Tell, that to morrow I with him wil fight,
And try in equall field, whether hath greater might.

XLIX
'But these conditions doe to him propound:
That if I vanquishe him, he shall obay
My law, and ever to my lore be bound;
And so will I, if me he vanquish may,
What ever he shall like to doe or say.
Goe streight, and take with thee, to witnesse it,
Sixe of thy fellowes of the best array,
And beare with you both wine and juncates fit,
And bid him eate; henceforth he oft shall hungry sit.'

L
The damzell streight obayd, and putting all
In readinesse, forth to the towne-gate went,
Where sounding loud a trumpet from the wall,
Unto those warlike knights she warning sent.
Then Talus, forth issuing from the tent,
Unto the wall his way did fearelesse take,
To weeten what that trumpets sounding ment:
Where that same damzell lowdly him bespake,
And shew'd that with his lord she would emparlaunce make.

LI
So he them streight conducted to his lord,
Who, as he could, them goodly well did greete,
Till they had told their message word by word:
Which he accepting well, as he could weete,
Them fairely entertaynd with curt'sies meete,
And gave them gifts and things of deare delight.

So backe againe they homeward turnd their feete.
But Artegall him selfe to rest did dight,
That he mote fresher be against the next daies fight.

CANTO V

Artegall fights with Radigund,
And is subdewd by guile:
He is by her emprisoned,
But wrought by Clarins wile.

I
So soone as day forth dawning from the East,
Nights humid curtaine from the heavens withdrew,
And earely calling forth both man and beast,
Comaunded them their daily workes renew,
These noble warriors, mindefull to pursew
The last daies purpose of their vowed fight,
Them selves thereto preparde in order dew;
The knight, as best was seeming for a knight,
And th' Amazon, as best it likt her selfe to dight:

II
All in a camis light of purple silke
Woven uppon with silver, subtly wrought,
And quilted uppon sattin white as milke,
Trayled with ribbands diversly distraught,
Like as the workeman had their courses taught;
Which was short tucked for light motion
Up to her ham, but, when she list, it raught
Downe to her lowest heele, and thereuppon
She wore for her defence a mayled habergeon.

III
And on her legs she painted buskins wore,
Basted with bends of gold on every side,
And mailes betweene, and laced close afore:
Uppon her thigh her cemitare was tide,
With an embrodered belt of mickell pride;
And on her shoulder hung her shield, bedeckt
Uppon the bosse with stones, that shined wide
As the faire moone in her most full aspect,
That to the moone it mote be like in each respect.

IV
So forth she came out of the citty gate,
With stately port and proud magnificence,

Guarded with many damzels, that did waite
Uppon her person for her sure defence,
Playing on shaumes and trumpets, that from hence
Their sound did reach unto the heavens hight.
So forth into the field she marched thence,
Where was a rich pavilion ready pight,
Her to receive, till time they should begin the fight.

V
Then forth came Artegall out of his tent,
All arm'd to point, and first the lists did enter:
Soone after eke came she, with fell intent,
And countenaunce fierce, as having fully bent her,
That battels utmost triall to adventer.
The lists were closed fast, to barre the rout
From rudely pressing to the middle center;
Which in great heapes them circled all about,
Wayting how fortune would resolve that daungerous dout.

VI
The trumpets sounded, and the field began;
With bitter strokes it both began and ended.
She at the first encounter on him ran
With furious rage, as if she had intended
Out of his breast the very heart have rended:
But he, that had like tempests often tride,
From that first flaw him selfe right well defended.
The more she rag'd, the more he did abide;
She hewd, she foynd, she lasht, she laid on every side.

VII
Yet still her blowes he bore, and her forbore,
Weening at last to win advantage new;
Yet still her crueltie increased more,
And though powre faild, her courage did accrew;
Which fayling, he gan fiercely her pursew.
Like as a smith that to his cunning feat
The stubborne mettall seeketh to subdew,
Soone as he feeles it mollifide with heat,
With his great yron sledge doth strongly on it beat.

VIII
So did Sir Artegall upon her lay,
As if she had an yron andvile beene,
That flakes of fire, bright as the sunny ray,
Out of her steely armes were flashing seene,
That all on fire ye would her surely weene.
But with her shield so well her selfe she warded
From the dread daunger of his weapon keene,
That all that while her life she safely garded:
But he that helpe from her against her will discarded.

IX
For with his trenchant blade at the next blow
Halfe of her shield he shared quite away,
That halfe her side it selfe did naked show,
And thenceforth unto daunger opened way.
Much was she moved with the mightie sway
Of that sad stroke, that halfe enrag'd she grew,
And like a greedie beare unto her pray,
With her sharpe cemitare at him she flew,
That glauncing downe his thigh, the purple bloud forth drew.

X
Thereat she gan to triumph with great boast,
And to upbrayd that chaunce which him misfell,
As if the prize she gotten had almost,
With spightfull speaches, fitting with her well;
That his great hart gan inwardly to swell
With indignation at her vaunting vaine,
And at her strooke with puissance fearefull fell;
Yet with her shield she warded it againe,
That shattered all to peeces round about the plaine.

XI
Having her thus disarmed of her shield,
Upon her helmet he againe her strooke,
That downe she fell upon the grassie field,
In sencelesse swoune, as if her life forsooke,
And pangs of death her spirit overtooke.
Whom when he saw before his foote prostrated,
He to her lept with deadly dreadfull looke,
And her sunshynie helmet soone unlaced,
Thinking at once both head and helmet to have raced.

XII
But when as he discovered had her face,
He saw, his senses straunge astonishment,
A miracle of Natures goodly grace
In her faire visage voide of ornament,
But bath'd in bloud and sweat together ment;
Which, in the rudenesse of that evill plight,
Bewrayd the signes of feature excellent:
Like as the moone, in foggie winters night,
Doth seeme to be her selfe, though darkned be her light.

XIII
At sight thereof his cruell minded hart
Empierced was with pittifull regard,
That his sharpe sword he threw from him apart,
Cursing his hand that had that visage mard:
No hand so cruell, nor no hart so hard,

But ruth of beautie will it mollifie.
By this upstarting from her swoune, she star'd
A while about her with confused eye;
Like one that from his dreame is waked suddenlye.

XIV
Soone as the knight she there by her did spy,
Standing with emptie hands all weaponlesse,
With fresh assault upon him she did fly,
And gan renew her former cruelnesse:
And though he still retyr'd, yet nathelesse
With huge redoubled strokes she on him layd;
And more increast her outrage mercilesse,
The more that he with meeke intreatie prayd,
Her wrathful hand from greedy vengeance to have stayd.

XV
Like as a puttocke having spyde in sight
A gentle faulcon sitting on an hill,
Whose other wing, now made unmeete for flight,
Was lately broken by some fortune ill;
The foolish kyte, led with licentious will,
Doth beat upon the gentle bird in vaine,
With many idle stoups her troubling still:
Even so did Radigund with bootlesse paine
Annoy this noble knight, and sorely him constraine.

XVI
Nought could he do, but shun the dred despight
Of her fierce wrath, and backward still retyre,
And with his single shield, well as he might,
Beare off the burden of her raging yre;
And evermore he gently did desyre
To stay her stroks, and he himselfe would yield:
Yet nould she hearke, ne let him once respyre,
Till he to her delivered had his shield,
And to her mercie him submitted in plaine field.

XVII
So was he overcome, not overcome,
But to her yeelded of his owne accord;
Yet was he justly damned by the doome
Of his owne mouth, that spake so warelesse word,
To be her thrall, and service her afford.
For though that he first victorie obtayned
Yet after, by abandoning his sword,
He wilfull lost that he before attayned.
No fayrer conquest then that with goodwill is gayned.

XVIII
Tho with her sword on him she flatling strooke,

In signe of true subjection to her powre,
And as her vassall him to thraldome tooke.
But Terpine, borne to' a more unhappy howre,
As he on whom the lucklesse starres did lowre,
She causd to be attacht, and forthwith led
Unto the crooke, t' abide the balefull stowre
From which he lately had through reskew fled:
Where he full shamefully was hanged by the hed.

XIX
But when they thought on Talus hands to lay,
He with his yron flaile amongst them thondred,
That they were fayne to let him scape away,
Glad from his companie to be so sondred;
Whose presence all their troups so much encombred,
That th' heapes of those which he did wound and slay,
Besides the rest dismayd, might not be nombred:
Yet all that while he would not once assay
To reskew his owne lord, but thought it just t' obay.

XX
Then tooke the Amazon this noble knight,
Left to her will by his owne wilfull blame,
And caused him to be disarmed quight
Of all the ornaments of knightly name,
With which whylome he gotten had great fame:
In stead whereof she made him to be dight
In womans weedes, that is to manhood shame,
And put before his lap a napron white,
In stead of curiets and bases fit for fight.

XXI
So being clad, she brought him from the field,
In which he had bene trayned many a day,
Into along large chamber, which was sield
With moniments of many knights decay,
By her subdewed in victorious fray:
Amongst the which she causd his warlike armes
Be hang'd on high, that mote his shame bewray;
And broke his sword, for feare of further harmes,
With which he wont to stirre up battailous alarmes.

XXII
There entred in, he round about him saw
Many brave knights, whose names right well he knew,
There bound t' obay that Amazons proud law,
Spinning and carding all in comely rew,
That his bigge hart loth'd so uncomely vew.
But they were forst, through penurie and pyne,
To doe those workes to them appointed dew:
For nought was given them to sup or dyne,

But what their hands could earne by twisting linnen twyne.

XXIII
Amongst them all she placed him most low,
And in his hand a distaffe to him gave,
That he thereon should spin both flax and tow;
A sordid office for a mind so brave:
So hard it is to be a womans slave.
Yet he it tooke in his owne selfes despight,
And thereto did himselfe right well behave,
Her to obay, sith he his faith had plight,
Her vassall to become, if she him wonne in fight.

XXIV
Who had him seene, imagine mote thereby
That whylome hath of Hercules bene told,
How for Iolas sake he did apply
His mightie hands the distaffe vile to hold,
For his huge club, which had subdew'd of old
So many monsters which the world annoyed;
His lyons skin chaungd to a pall of gold,
In which, forgetting warres, he onely joyed
In combats of sweet love, and with his mistresse toyed.

XXV
Such is the crueltie of women kynd,
When they have shaken off the shamefast band,
With which wise Nature did them strongly bynd,
T' obay the heasts of mans well ruling hand,
That then all rule and reason they withstand,
To purchase a licentious libertie.
But vertuous women wisely understand,
That they were borne to base humilitie,
Unlesse the heavens them lift to lawfull soveraintie.

XXVI
Thus there long while continu'd Artegall,
Serving proud Radigund with true subjection;
How ever it his noble heart did gall
T' obay a womans tyrannous direction,
That might have had of life or death election:
But having chosen, now he might not chaunge.
During which time, the warlike Amazon,
Whose wandring fancie after lust did raunge,
Gan cast a secret liking to this captive straunge.

XXVII
Which long concealing in her covert brest,
She chaw'd the cud of lovers carefull plight;
Yet could it not so thoroughly digest,
Being fast fixed in her wounded spright,

But it tormented her both day and night:
Yet would she not thereto yeeld free accord,
To serve the lowly vassall of her might,
And of her servant make her soverayne lord:
So great her pride, that she such basenesse much abhord.

XXVIII
So much the greater still her anguish grew,
Through stubborne handling of her love-sicke hart;
And still the more she strove it to subdew,
The more she still augmented her owne smart,
And wyder made the wound of th' hidden dart.
At last, when long she struggled had in vaine,
She gan to stoupe, and her proud mind convert
To meeke obeysance of Loves mightie raine,
And him entreat for grace, that had procur'd her paine.

XXIX
Unto her selfe in secret she did call
Her nearest handmayd, whom she most did trust,
And to her said: 'Clarinda, whom of all
I trust a live, sith I thee fostred first;
Now is the time that I untimely must
Thereof make tryall, in my greatest need:
It is so hapned that the heavens unjust,
Spighting my happie freedome, have agreed
To thrall my looser life, or my last bale to breed.'

XXX
With that she turn'd her head, as halfe abashed,
To hide the blush which in her visage rose,
And through her eyes like sudden lightning flashed,
Decking her cheeke with a vermilion rose:
But soone she did her countenance compose,
And to her turning, thus began againe:
'This griefes deepe wound I would to thee disclose,
Thereto compelled through hart-murdring paine,
But dread of shame my doubtfull lips doth still restraine.'

XXXI
'Ah! my deare dread,' said then the faithfull mayd,
'Can dread of ought your dreadlesse hart withhold,
That many hath with dread of death dismayd,
And dare even deathes most dreadfull face behold?
Say on, my soverayne ladie, and be bold:
Doth not your handmayds life at your foot lie?'
Therewith much comforted, she gan unfold
The cause of her conceived maladie,
As one that would confesse, yet faine would it denie.

XXXII

'Clarin,' sayd she, 'thou seest yond Fayry knight,
Whom not my valour, but his owne brave mind
Subjected hath to my unequall might:
What right is it, that he should thraldome find,
For lending life to me, a wretch unkind,
That for such good him recompence with ill?
Therefore I cast how I may him unbind,
And by his freedome get his free goodwill;
Yet so, as bound to me he may continue still:

XXXIII
'Bound unto me, but not with such hard bands
Of strong compulsion and streight violence,
As now in miserable state he stands;
But with sweet love and sure benevolence,
Voide of malitious mind or foule offence.
To which if thou canst win him any way,
Without discoverie of my thoughts pretence,
Both goodly meede of him it purchase may,
And eke with gratefull service me right well apay.

XXXIV
'Which that thou mayst the better bring to pas,
Loe here this ring, which shall thy warrant bee,
And token true to old Eumenias,
From time to time, when thou it best shalt see,
That in and out thou mayst have passage free.
Goe now, Clarinda; well thy wits advise,
And all thy forces gather unto thee,
Armies of lovely lookes, and speeches wise,
With which thou canst even Jove himselfe to love entise.'

XXXV
The trustie mayd, conceiving her intent,
Did with sure promise of her good indevour
Give her great comfort and some harts content.
So from her parting, she thenceforth did labour
By all the meanes she might, to curry favour
With th' Elfin knight, her ladies best beloved:
With daily shew of courteous kind behaviour,
Even at the markewhite of his hart she roved,
And with wide glauncing words, one day she thus him proved:

XXXVI
'Unhappie knight, upon whose hopelesse state
Fortune, envying good, hath felly frowned,
And cruell heavens have heapt an heavy fate;
I rew that thus thy better dayes are drowned
In sad despaire, and all thy senses swowned
In stupid sorow, sith thy juster merit
Might else have with felicitie bene crowned:

Looke up at last, and wake thy dulled spirit,
To thinke how this long death thou mightest disinherit.'

XXXVII
Much did he marvell at her uncouth speach,
Whose hidden drift he could not well perceive;
And gan to doubt, least she him sought t' appeach
Of treason, or some guilefull traine did weave,
Through which she might his wretched life bereave.
Both which to barre, he with this answere met her:
'Faire damzell, that with ruth (as I perceave)
Of my mishaps, art mov'd to wish me better,
For such your kind regard I can but rest your detter.

XXXVIII
'Yet weet ye well, that to a courage great
It is no lesse beseeming well, to beare
The storme of Fortunes frowne, or Heavens threat,
Then in the sunshine of her countenance cleare
Timely to joy and carrie comely cheare.
For though this cloud have now me overcast,
Yet doe I not of better times despeyre;
And, though unlike, they should for ever last,
Yet in my truthes assurance I rest fixed fast.'

XXXIX
'But what so stonie mind,' she then replyde,
'But, if in his owne powre occasion lay,
Would to his hope a windowe open wyde,
And to his fortunes helpe make readie way?'
'Unworthy sure,' quoth he, 'of better day,
That will not take the offer of good hope,
And eke pursew, if he attaine it may.'
Which speaches she applying to the scope
Of her intent, this further purpose to him shope:

XL
'Then why doest not, thou ill advized man,
Make meanes to win thy libertie forlorne,
And try if thou by faire entreatie can
Move Radigund? who, though she still have worne
Her dayes in warre, yet (weet thou) was not borne
Of beares and tygres, nor so salvage mynded,
As that, albe all love of men she scorne,
She yet forgets that she of men was kynded:
And sooth oft seene, that proudest harts base love hath blynded.'

XLI
'Certes, Clarinda, not of cancred will,'
Sayd he, 'nor obstinate disdainefull mind,
I have forbore this duetie to fulfill:

For well I may this weene, by that I fynd,
That she, a queene, and come of princely kynd,
Both worthie is for to be sewd unto,
Chiefely by him whose life her law doth bynd,
And eke of powre her owne doome to undo,
And als' of princely grace to be inclyn'd thereto.

XLII
'But want of meanes hath bene mine onely let
From seeking favour, where it doth abound;
Which if I might by your good office get,
I to your selfe should rest for ever bound,
And readie to deserve what grace I found.'
She feeling him thus bite upon the bayt,
Yet doubting least his hold was but unsound,
And not well fastened, would not strike him strayt,
But drew him on with hope, fit leasure to awayt.

XLIII
But foolish mayd! whyles, heedlesse of the hooke,
She thus oft times was beating off and on,
Through slipperie footing fell into the brooke,
And there was caught to her confusion.
For seeking thus to salve the Amazon,
She wounded was with her deceipts owne dart,
And gan thenceforth to cast affection,
Conceived close in her beguiled hart,
To Artegall, through pittie of his causelesse smart.

XLIV
Yet durst she not disclose her fancies wound,
Ne to himselfe, for doubt of being sdayned,
Ne yet to any other wight on ground,
For feare her mistresse shold have knowledge gayned,
But to her selfe it secretly retayned,
Within the closet of her covert brest:
The more thereby her tender hart was payned.
Yet to awayt fit time she weened best,
And fairely did dissemble her sad thoughts unrest.

XLV
One day her ladie, calling her apart,
Gan to demaund of her some tydings good,
Touching her loves successe, her lingring smart.
Therewith she gan at first to change her mood,
As one adaw'd, and halfe confused stood;
But quickly she it overpast, so soone
As she her face had wypt, to fresh her blood:
Tho gan she tell her all that she had donne,
And all the wayes she sought, his love for to have wonne:

XLVI

But sayd, that he was obstinate and sterne,
Scorning her offers and conditions vaine;
Ne would be taught with any termes to lerne
So fond a lesson as to love againe.
Die rather would he in penurious paine,
And his abridged dayes in dolour wast,
Then his foes love or liking entertaine:
His resolution was, both first and last,
His bodie was her thrall, his hart was freely plast.

XLVII

Which when the cruell Amazon perceived,
She gan to storme, and rage, and rend her gall,
For very fell despight, which she conceived,
To be so scorned of a base borne thrall,
Whose life did lie in her least eye-lids fall;
Of which she vow'd with many a cursed threat,
That she therefore would him ere long forstall.
Nathlesse, when calmed was her furious heat,
She chang'd that threatfull mood, and mildly gan entreat:

XLVIII

'What now is left, Clarinda? what remaines,
That we may compasse this our enterprize?
Great shame to lose so long employed paines,
And greater shame t' abide so great misprize,
With which he dares our offers thus despize.
Yet that his guilt the greater may appeare,
And more my gratious mercie by this wize,
I will a while with his first folly beare,
Till thou have tride againe, and tempted him more neare.

XLIX

'Say and do all that may thereto prevaile;
Leave nought unpromist that may him perswade,
Life, freedome, grace, and gifts of great availe,
With which the gods themselves are mylder made:
Thereto adde art, even womens wittie trade,
The art of mightie words, that men can charme;
With which in case thou canst him not invade,
Let him feele hardnesse of thy heavie arme:
Who will not stoupe with good shall be made stoupe with harme.

L

'Some of his diet doe from him withdraw;
For I him find to be too proudly fed:
Give him more labour, and with streighter law,
That he with worke may be forwearied:
Let him lodge hard, and lie in strawen bed,
That may pull downe the courage of his pride;

And lay upon him, for his greater dread,
Cold yron chaines, with which let him be tide;
And let what ever he desires be him denide.

LI
'When thou hast all this doen, then bring me newes
Of his demeane: thenceforth not like a lover,
But like a rebell stout I will him use.
For I resolve this siege not to give over,
Till I the conquest of my will recover.'
So she departed, full of griefe and sdaine,
Which inly did to great impatience move her.
But the false mayden shortly turn'd againe
Unto the prison, where her hart did thrall remaine.

LII
There all her subtill nets she did unfold,
And all the engins of her wit display;
In which she meant him warelesse to enfold,
And of his innocence to make her pray.
So cunningly she wrought her crafts assay,
That both her ladie, and her selfe withall,
And eke the knight attonce she did betray:
But most the knight, whom she with guilefull call
Did cast for to allure, into her trap to fall.

LIII
As a bad nurse, which, fayning to receive
In her owne mouth the food ment for her chyld,
Withholdes it to her selfe, and doeth deceive
The infant, so for want of nourture spoyld:
Even so Clarinda her owne dame beguyld,
And turn'd the trust which was in her affyde
To feeding of her private fire, which boyld
Her inward brest, and in her entrayles fryde,
The more that she it sought to cover and to hyde.

LIV
For comming to this knight, she purpose fayned,
How earnest suit she earst for him had made
Unto her queene, his freedome to have gayned;
But by no meanes could her thereto perswade:
But that, in stead thereof, she sternly bade
His miserie to be augmented more,
And many yron bands on him to lade;
All which nathlesse she for his love forbore:
So praying him t' accept her service evermore.

LV
And more then that, she promist that she would,
In case she might finde favour in his eye,

Devize how to enlarge him out of hould.
The Fayrie, glad to gaine his libertie,
Can yeeld great thankes for such her curtesie;
And with faire words, fit for the time and place,
To feede the humour of her maladie,
Promist, if she would free him from that case,
He wold, by all good means he might, deserve such grace.

LVI
So daily he faire semblant did her shew,
Yet never meant he in his noble mind,
To his owne absent love to be untrew:
Ne ever did deceiptfull Clarin find
In her false hart, his bondage to unbind;
But rather how she mote him faster tye.
Therefore unto her mistresse most unkind
She daily told, her love he did defye,
And him she told, her dame his freedome did denye.

LVII
Yet thus much friendship she to him did show,
That his scarse diet somewhat was amended,
And his worke lessened, that his love mote grow:
Yet to her dame him still she discommended,
That she with him mote be the more offended.
Thus he long while in thraldome there remayned,
Of both beloved well, but litle frended;
Untill his owne true love his freedome gayned,
Which in an other canto will be best contayned.

CANTO VI

Talus brings newes to Britomart
Of Artegals mishap:
She goes to seeke him, Dolon meetes,
Who seekes her to entrap.

I
Some men, I wote, will deeme in Artegall
Great weaknesse, and report of him much ill,
For yeelding so himselfe a wretched thrall
To th' insolent commaund of womens will;
That all his former praise doth fowly spill.
But he the man, that say or doe so dare,
Be well adviz'd that he stand stedfast still:
For never yet was wight so well aware,
But he at first or last was trapt in womens snare.

II
Yet in the streightnesse of that captive state,
This gentle knight himselfe so well behaved,
That notwithstanding all the subtill bait,
With which those Amazons his love still craved,
To his owne love his loialtie he saved:
Whose character in th' adamantine mould
Of his true hart so firmely was engraved,
That no new loves impression ever could
Bereave it thence: such blot his honour blemish should.

III
Yet his owne love, the noble Britomart,
Scarse so conceived in her jealous thought,
What time sad tydings of his balefull smart
In womans bondage Talus to her brought
Brought in untimely houre, ere it was sought.
For after that the utmost date, assynde
For his returne, she waited had for nought,
She gan to cast in her misdoubtfull mynde
A thousand feares, that love-sicke fancies faine to fynde.

IV
Sometime she feared, least some hard mishap
Had him misfalne in his adventurous quest;
Sometime least his false foe did him entrap
In traytrous traine, or had unwares opprest:
But most she did her troubled mynd molest,
And secretly afflict with jealous feare,
Least some new love had him from her possest;
Yet loth she was, since she no ill did heare,
To thinke of him so ill: yet could she not forbeare.

V
One while she blam'd her selfe; another whyle
She him condemn'd, as trustlesse and untrew:
And then, her griefe with errour to beguyle,
She fayn'd to count the time againe anew,
As if before she had not counted trew.
For houres but dayes; for weekes, that passed were,
She told but moneths, to make them seeme more few:
Yet when she reckned them, still drawing neare,
Each hour did seeme a moneth, and every moneth a yeare.

VI
But when as yet she saw him not returne,
She thought to send some one to seeke him out;
But none she found so fit to serve that turne,
As her owne selfe, to ease her selfe of dout.
Now she deviz'd, amongst the warlike rout

Of errant knights, to seeke her errant knight;
And then againe resolv'd to hunt him out
Amongst loose ladies, lapped in delight:
And then both knights envide, and ladies eke did spight.

VII
One day, when as she long had sought for ease
In every place, and every place thought best,
Yet found no place that could her liking please,
She to a window came, that opened west,
Towards which coast her love his way addrest.
There looking forth, shee in her heart did find
Many vaine fancies, working her unrest;
And sent her winged thoughts, more swift then wind,
To beare unto her love the message of her mind.

VIII
There as she looked long, at last she spide
One comming towards her with hasty speede:
Well weend she then, ere him she plaine descride,
That it was one sent from her love indeede.
Who when he nigh approcht, shee mote arede
That it was Talus, Artegall his groome;
Whereat her heart was fild with hope and drede;
Ne would she stay till he in place could come,
But ran to meete him forth, to know his tidings somme.

IX
Even in the dore him meeting, she begun:
'And where is he thy lord, and how far hence?
Declare at once; and hath he lost or wun?'
The yron man, albe he wanted sence
And sorrowes feelings, yet with conscience
Of his ill newes, did inly chill and quake,
And stood still mute, as one in great suspence,
As if that by his silence he would make
Her rather reade his meaning, then him selfe it spake.

X
Till she againe thus sayd: 'Talus, be bold,
And tell what ever it be, good or bad,
That from thy tongue thy hearts intent doth hold.'
To whom he thus at length: 'The tidings sad,
That I would hide, will needs, I see, be rad.
My lord, your love, by hard mishap doth lie
In wretched bondage, wofully bestad.'
'Ay me,' quoth she, 'what wicked destinie!
And is he vanquisht by his tyrant enemy?'

XI
'Not by that tyrant, his intended foe;

But by a tyrannesse,' he then replide,
'That him captived hath in haplesse woe.'
'Cease, thou bad newes-man; badly doest thou hide
Thy maisters shame, in harlots bondage tide.
The rest my selfe too readily can spell.'
With that in rage she turn'd from him aside,
Forcing in vaine the rest to her to tell,
And to her chamber went like solitary cell.

XII
There she began to make her monefull plaint
Against her knight, for being so untrew;
And him to touch with falshoods fowle at-taint,
That all his other honour overthrew.
Oft did she blame her selfe, and often rew,
For yeelding to a straungers love so light,
Whose life and manners straunge she never knew;
And evermore she did him sharpely twight
For breach of faith to her, which he had firmely plight.

XIII
And then she in her wrathfull will did cast,
How to revenge that blot of honour blent;
To fight with him, and goodly die her last:
And then againe she did her selfe torment,
Inflicting on her selfe his punishment.
A while she walkt, and chauft; a while she threw
Her selfe uppon her bed, and did lament:
Yet did she not lament with loude alew,
As women wont, but with deepe sighes, and singulfs few.

XIV
Like as a wayward childe, whose sounder sleepe
Is broken with some fearefull dreames affright,
With froward will doth set him selfe to weepe;
Ne can be stild for all his nurses might,
But kicks, and squals, and shriekes for fell despight;
Now scratching her, and her loose locks misusing;
Now seeking darkenesse, and now seeking light;
Then craving sucke, and then the sucke refusing:
Such was this ladies, fit, in her loves fond accusing.

XV
But when she had with such unquiet fits
Her selfe there close afflicted long in vaine,
Yet found no easement in her troubled wits,
She unto Talus forth return'd againe,
By change of place seeking to ease her paine;
And gan enquire of him, with mylder, mood,
The certaine cause of Artegals detaine;
And what he did, and in what state he stood,

And whether he did woo, or whether he were woo'd.

XVI
'Ah wellaway!' sayd then the yron man,
'That he is not the while in state to woo;
But lies in wretched thraldome, weake and wan,
Not by strong hand compelled thereunto,
But his owne doome, that none can now undoo.'
'Sayd I not then,' quoth shee, 'erwhile aright,
That this is thinge compacte betwixt you two,
Me to deceive of faith unto me plight,
Since that he was not forst, nor overcome in fight?'

XVII
With that he gan at large to her dilate
The whole discourse of his captivance sad,
In sort as ye have heard the same of late.
All which when she with hard enduraunce had
Heard to the end, she was right sore bestad,
With sodaine stounds of wrath and griefe attone:
Ne would abide, till she had aunswere made,
But streight her selfe did dight, and armor don;
And mounting to her steede, bad Talus guide her on.

XVIII
So forth she rode uppon her ready way,
To seeke her knight, as Talus her did guide:
Sadly she rode, and never word did say,
Nor good nor bad, ne ever lookt aside,
But still right downe, and in her thought did hide
The felnesse of her heart, right fully bent
To fierce avengement of that womans pride,
Which had her lord in her base prison pent,
And so great honour with so fowle reproch had blent.

XIX
So as she thus melancholicke did ride,
Chawing the cud of griefe and inward paine,
She chaunst to meete toward the even-tide
A knight, that softly paced on the plaine,
As if him selfe to solace he were faine.
Well shot in yeares he seem'd, and rather bent
To peace, then needlesse trouble to constraine;
As well by view of that his vestiment,
As by his modest semblant, that no evill ment.

XX
He, comming neare, gan gently her salute
With curteous words, in the most comely wize;
Who though desirous rather to rest mute,
Then termes to entertaine of common guize,

Yet rather then she kindnesse would despize,
She would her selfe displease, so him requite.
Then gan the other further to devize
Of things abrode, as next to hand did light,
And many things demaund, to which she answer'd light.

XXI
For little lust had she to talke of ought,
Or ought to heare, that mote delightfull bee;
Her minde was whole possessed of one thought,
That gave none other place. Which when as hee
By outward signes (as well he might) did see,
He list no lenger to use lothfull speach,
But her besought to take it well in gree,
Sith shady dampe had dimd the heavens reach,
To lodge with him that night, unles good cause empeach.

XXII
The championesse, now seeing night at dore,
Was glad to yeeld unto his good request:
And with him went without gaine-saying more.
Not farre away, but little wide by west,
His dwelling was, to which he him addrest;
Where soone arriving, they received were
In seemely wise, as them beseemed best:
For he their host them goodly well did cheare,
And talk't of pleasant things, the night away to weare.

XXIII
Thus passing th' evening well, till time of rest,
Then Britomart unto a bowre was brought;
Where groomes awayted her to have undrest.
But she ne would undressed be for ought,
Ne doffe her armes, though he her much besought.
For she had vow'd, she sayd, not to forgo
Those warlike weedes, till she revenge had wrought
Of a late wrong uppon a mortall foe;
Which she would sure performe, betide her wele or wo.

XXIV
Which when their host perceiv'd, right discontent
In minde he grew, for feare least by that art
He should his purpose misse, which close he ment:
Yet taking leave of her, he did depart.
There all that night remained Britomart,
Restlesse, recomfortlesse, with heart deepe grieved,
Not suffering the least twinckling sleepe to start
Into her eye, which th' heart mote have relieved,
But if the least appear'd, her eyes she streight reprieved.

XXV

'Ye guilty eyes,' sayd she, 'the which with guyle
My heart at first betrayd, will ye betray
My life now to, for which a little whyle
Ye will not watch? False watches, well-away!
I wote when ye did watch both night and day
Unto your losse: and now needes will ye sleepe?
Now ye have made my heart to wake alway,
Now will ye sleepe? ah! wake, and rather weepe,
To thinke of your nights want, that should yee waking keepe.'

XXVI

Thus did she watch, and weare the weary night
In waylfull plaints, that none was to appease;
Now walking soft, now sitting still upright,
As sundry chaunge her seemed best to ease.
Ne lesse did Talus suffer sleepe to seaze
His eye-lids sad, but watcht continually,
Lying without her dore in great disease;
Like to a spaniell wayting carefully,
Least any should betray his lady treacherously.

XXVII

What time the native belman of the night,
The bird that warned Peter of his fall,
First rings his silver bell t' each sleepy wight,
That should their mindes up to devotion call,
She heard a wondrous noise below the hall.
All sodainely the bed, where she should lie,
By a false trap was let adowne to fall
Into a lower roome, and by and by
The loft was raysd againe, that no man could it spie.

XXVIII

With sight whereof she was dismayd right sore,
Perceiving well the treason which was ment:
Yet stirred not at all for doubt of more,
But kept her place with courage confident,
Wayting what would ensue of that event.
It was not long before she heard the sound
Of armed men, comming with close intent
Towards her chamber; at which dreadfull stound
She quickly caught her sword, and shield about her bound.

XXIX

With that there came unto her chamber dore
Two knights, all armed ready for to fight,
And after them full many other more,
A raskall rout, with weapons rudely dight.
Whom soone as Talus spide by glims of night,
He started up, there where on ground he lay,
And in his hand his thresher ready keight.

They seeing that, let drive at him streight way,
And round about him preace in riotous aray.

XXX
But soone as he began to lay about
With his rude yron flaile, they gan to flie,
Both armed knights and eke unarmed rout:
Yet Talus after them apace did plie,
Where ever in the darke he could them spie;
That here and there like scattred sheepe they lay.
Then backe returning, where his dame did lie,
He to her told the story of that fray,
And all that treason there intended did bewray.

XXXI
Wherewith though wondrous wroth, and inly burning
To be avenged for so fowle a deede,
Yet being forst to abide the daies returning,
She there remain'd, but with right wary heede,
Least any more such practise should proceede.
Now mote ye know (that which to Britomart
Unknowen was) whence all this did proceede,
And for what cause so great mischievous smart
Was ment to her, that never evill ment in hart.

XXXII
The goodman of this house was Dolon hight,
A man of subtill wit and wicked minde,
That whilome in his youth had bene a knight,
And armes had borne, but little good could finde,
And much lesse honour by that warlike kinde
Of life: for he was nothing valorous,
But with slie shiftes and wiles did underminde
All noble knights which were adventurous,
And many brought to shame by treason treacherous.

XXXIII
He had three sonnes, all three like fathers sonnes,
Like treacherous, like full of fraud and guile,
Of all that on this earthly compasse wonnes:
The eldest of the which was slaine erewhile
By Artegall, through his owne guilty wile;
His name was Guizor; whose untimely fate
For to avenge, full many treasons vile
His father Dolon had deviz'd of late
With these his wicked sons, and shewd his cankred hate.

XXXIV
For sure he weend that this his present guest
Was Artegall, by many tokens plaine;
But chiefly by that yron page he ghest,

Which still was wont with Artegall remaine;
And therefore ment him surely to have slaine.
But by Gods grace, and her good heedinesse,
She was preserved from their traytrous traine.
Thus she all night wore out in watchfulnesse,
Ne suffred slothfull sleepe her eyelids to oppresse.

XXXV
The morrow next, so soone as dawning houre
Discovered had the light to living eye,
She forth yssew'd out of her loathed bowre,
With full intent t' avenge that villany
On that vilde man and all his family:
And comming down to seeke them where they wond,
Nor sire, nor sonnes, nor any could she spie:
Each rowme she sought, but them all empty fond:
They all were fled for feare, but whether, nether kond.

XXXVI
She saw it vaine to make there lenger stay,
But tooke her steede, and thereon mounting light,
Gan her addresse unto her former way.
She had not rid the mountenance of a flight,
But that she saw there present in her sight
Those two false brethren, on that perillous bridge
On which Pollente with Artegall did fight.
Streight was the passage like a ploughed ridge,
That, if two met, the one mote needes fall over the lidge.

XXXVII
There they did thinke them selves on her to wreake:
Who as she nigh unto them drew, the one
These vile reproches gan unto her speake:
'Thou recreant false traytor, that with lone
Of armes hast knighthood stolne, yet knight art none,
No more shall now the darkenesse of the night
Defend thee from the vengeance of thy fone,
But with thy bloud thou shalt appease the spright
Of Guizor, by thee slaine, and murdred by thy slight.'

XXXVIII
Strange were the words in Britomartis eare;
Yet stayd she not for them, but forward fared,
Till to the perillous bridge she came, and there
Talus desir'd that he might have prepared
The way to her, and those two losels scared.
But she thereat was wroth, that for despight
The glauncing sparkles through her bever glared,
And from her eies did flash out fiery light,
Like coles that through a silver censer sparkle bright.

XXXIX
She stayd not to advise which way to take;
But putting spurres unto her fiery beast,
Thorough the midst of them she way did make.
The one of them, which most her wrath increast,
Uppon her speare she bore before her breast,
Till to the bridges further end she past,
Where falling downe, his challenge he releast:
The other over side the bridge she cast
Into the river, where he drunke his deadly last.

XL
As when the flashing levin haps to light
Uppon two stubborne oakes, which stand so neare
That way betwixt them none appeares in sight;
The engin fiercely flying forth, doth teare
Th' one from the earth, and through the aire doth beare;
The other it with force doth overthrow
Uppon one side, and from his rootes doth reare:
So did the Championesse those two there strow,
And to their sire their carcasses left to bestow.

CANTO VII

Britomart comes to Isis Church,
Where shee strange visions sees:
She fights with Radigund, her slaies,
And Artegall thence frees.

I
Nought is on earth more sacred or divine,
That gods and men doe equally adore,
Then this same vertue that doth right define:
For th' hevens themselves, whence mortal men implore
Right in their wrongs, are rul'd by righteous lore
Of highest Jove, who doth true justice deale
To his inferiour gods, and evermore
Therewith contains his heavenly commonweale:
The skill whereof to princes hearts he doth reveale.

II
Well therefore did the antique world invent,
That Justice was a god of soveraine grace,
And altars unto him, and temples lent,
And heavenly honours in the highest place;
Calling him great Osyris, of the race
Of th' old Ægyptian kings, that whylome were;
With fayned colours shading a true case:

For that Osyris, whilest he lived here,
The justest man alive and truest did appeare.

III
His wife was Isis, whom they likewise made
A goddesse of great powre and soverainty,
And in her person cunningly did shade
That part of justice which is equity,
Whereof I have to treat here presently.
Unto whose temple when as Britomart
Arrived, shee with great humility
Did enter in, ne would that night depart;
But Talus mote not be admitted to her part.

IV
There she received was in goodly wize
Of many priests, which duely did attend
Uppon the rites and daily sacrifize,
All clad in linnen robes with silver hemd;
And on their heads, with long locks comely kemd,
They wore rich mitres shaped like the moone,
To shew that Isis doth the moone portend;
Like as Osyris signifies the sunne:
For that they both like race in equall justice runne.

V
The championesse them greeting, as she could,
Was thence by them into the temple led;
Whose goodly building when she did behould,
Borne uppon stately pillours, all dispred
With shining gold, and arched over hed,
She wondred at the workemans passing skill,
Whose like before she never saw nor red;
And thereuppon long while stood gazing still,
But thought that she thereon could never gaze her fill.

VI
Thence forth unto the idoll they her brought,
The which was framed all of silver fine,
So well as could with cunning hand be wrought,
And clothed all in garments made of line,
Hemd all about with fringe of silver twine.
Uppon her head she wore a crowne of gold,
To shew that she had powre in things divine;
And at her feete a crocodile was rold,
That with his wreathed taile her middle did enfold.

VII
One foote was set uppon the crocodile,
And on the ground the other fast did stand,
So meaning to suppresse both forged guile

And open force: and in her other hand
She stretched forth a long white sclender wand.
Such was the goddesse; whom when Britomart
Had long beheld, her selfe uppon the land
She did prostrate, and with right humble hart,
Unto her selfe her silent prayers did impart.

VIII
To which the idoll as it were inclining,
Her wand did move with amiable looke,
By outward shew her inward sence desining.
Who well perceiving how her wand she shooke,
It as a token of good fortune tooke.
By this the day with dampe was overcast,
And joyous light the house of Jove forsooke:
Which when she saw, her helmet she unlaste,
And by the altars side her selfe to slumber plaste.

IX
For other beds the priests there used none,
But on their mother Earths deare lap did lie,
And bake their sides uppon the cold hard stone,
T' enure them selves to sufferaunce thereby
And proud rebellious flesh to mortify.
For, by the vow of their religion,
They tied were to stedfast chastity,
And continence of life, that, all forgon,
They mote the better tend to their devotion.

X
Therefore they mote not taste of fleshly food,
Ne feed on ought the which doth bloud containe,
Ne drinke of wine, for wine they say is blood,
Even the bloud of gyants, which were slaine
By thundring Jove in the Phlegrean plaine:
For which the Earth (as they the story tell)
Wroth with the gods, which to perpetuall paine
Had damn'd her sonnes, which gainst them did rebell,
With inward griefe and malice did against them swell.

XI
And of their vitall bloud, the which was shed
Into her pregnant bosome, forth she brought
The fruitfull vine, whose liquor blouddy red,
Having the mindes of men with fury fraught,
Mote in them stirre up old rebellious thought,
To make new warre against the gods againe:
Such is the powre of that same fruit, that nought
The fell contagion may thereof restraine,
Ne within reasons rule her madding mood containe.

XII

There did the warlike maide her selfe repose,
Under the wings of Isis all that night,
And with sweete rest her heavy eyes did close,
After that long daies toile and weary plight.
Where whilest her earthly parts with soft delight
Of sencelesse sleepe did deeply drowned lie,
There did appeare unto her heavenly spright
A wondrous vision, which did close implie
The course of all her fortune and posteritie.

XIII

Her seem'd, as she was doing sacrifize
To Isis, deckt with mitre on her hed
And linnen stole, after those priestes guize,
All sodainely she saw transfigured
Her linnen stole to robe of scarlet red,
And moone-like mitre to a crowne of gold,
That even she her selfe much wondered
At such a chaunge, and joyed to behold
Her selfe adorn'd with gems and jewels manifold.

XIV

And in the midst of her felicity,
An hideous tempest seemed from below
To rise through all the temple sodainely,
That from the altar all about did blow
The holy fire, and all the embers strow
Uppon the ground, which, kindled privily,
Into outragious flames unwares did grow,
That all the temple put in jeopardy
Of flaming, and her selfe in great perplexity.

XV

With that the crocodile, which sleeping lay
Under the idols feete in fearelesse bowre,
Seem'd to awake in horrible dismay,
As being troubled with that stormy stowre;
And gaping greedy wide, did streight devoure
Both flames and tempest: with which growen great,
And swolne with pride of his owne peerelesse powre,
He gan to threaten her likewise to eat;
But that the goddesse with her rod him backe did beat.

XVI

Tho turning all his pride to humblesse meeke,
Him selfe before her feete he lowly threw,
And gan for grace and love of her to seeke:
Which she accepting, he so neare her drew,
That of his game she soone enwombed grew,
And forth did bring a lion of great might;

That shortly did all other beasts subdew.
With that she waked, full of fearefull fright,
And doubtfully dismayd through that so uncouth sight.

XVII
So thereuppon long while she musing lay,
With thousand thoughts feeding her fantasie,
Untill she spide the lampe of lightsome day,
Up-lifted in the porch of heaven hie.
Then up she rose fraught with melancholy,
And forth into the lower parts did pas;
Whereas the priestes she found full busily
About their holy things for morrow mas:
Whom she saluting faire, faire resaluted was.

XVIII
But, by the change of her unchearefull looke,
They might perceive she was not well in plight;
Or that some pensivenesse to heart she tooke.
Therefore thus one of them, who seem'd in sight
To be the greatest and the gravest wight,
To her bespake: 'Sir knight, it seemes to me,
That, thorough evill rest of this last night,
Or ill apayd or much dismayd ye be,
That by your change of cheare is easie for to see.'

XIX
'Certes,' sayd she, 'sith ye so well have spide
The troublous passion of my pensive mind,
I will not seeke the same from you to hide,
But will my cares unfolde, in hope to find
Your aide, to guide me out of errour blind.'
'Say on,' quoth he, 'the secret of your hart:
For by the holy vow which me doth bind
I am adjur'd, best counsell to impart
To all that shall require my comfort in their smart.'

XX
Then gan she to declare the whole discourse
Of all that vision which to her appeard,
As well as to her minde it had recourse.
All which when he unto the end had heard,
Like to a weake faint-hearted man he fared,
Through great astonishment of that strange sight;
And with long locks up-standing, stifly stared
Like one adawed with some dreadfull spright.
So fild with heavenly fury, thus he her behight:

XXI
'Magnificke virgin, that in queint disguise
Of British armes doest maske thy royall blood,

So to pursue a perillous emprize,
How couldst thou weene, through that disguized hood,
To hide thy state from being understood?
Can from th' immortall gods ought hidden bee?
They doe thy linage, and thy lordly brood,
They doe thy sire, lamenting sore for thee,
They doe thy love, forlorne in womens thraldome, see.

XXII
'The end whereof, and all the long event,
They doe to thee in this same dreame discover.
For that same crocodile doth represent
The righteous knight that is thy faithfull lover,
Like to Osyris in all just endever.
For that same crocodile Osyris is,
That under Isis feete doth sleepe for ever:
To shew that clemence oft, in things amis,
Restraines those sterne behests and cruell doomes of his.

XXIII
'That knight shall all the troublous stormes asswage,
And raging flames, that many foes shall reare,
To hinder thee from the just heritage
Of thy sires crowne, and from thy countrey deare.
Then shalt thou take him to thy loved fere,
And joyne in equall portion of thy realme:
And afterwards a sonne to him shalt beare,
That lion-like shall shew his powre extreame.
So blesse thee God, and give thee joyance of thy dreame.'

XXIV
All which when she unto the end had heard,
She much was eased in her troublous thought,
And on those priests bestowed rich reward:
And royall gifts of gold and silver wrought
She for a present to their goddesse brought.
Then taking leave of them, she forward went,
To seeke her love, where he was to be sought;
Ne rested till she came without relent
Unto the land of Amazons, as she was bent.

XXV
Whereof when newes to Radigund was brought,
Not with amaze, as women wonted bee,
She was confused in her troublous thought,
But fild with courage and with joyous glee,
As glad to heare of armes, the which now she
Had long surceast, she bad to open bold,
That she the face of her new foe might see.
But when they of that yron man had told,
Which late her folke had slaine, she bad them forth to hold.

XXVI
So there without the gate (as seemed best)
She caused her pavilion be pight;
In which stout Britomart her selfe did rest,
Whiles Talus watched at the dore all night.
All night likewise, they of the towne in fright
Uppon their wall good watch and ward did keepe.
The morrow next, so soone as dawning light
Bad doe away the dampe of drouzie sleepe,
The warlike Amazon out of her bowre did peepe;

XXVII
And caused streight a trumpet loud to shrill,
To warne her foe to battell soone be prest:
Who, long before awoke, (for she ful ill
Could sleepe all night, that in unquiet brest
Did closely harbour such a jealous guest)
Was to the battell whilome ready dight.
Eftsoones that warriouresse with haughty crest
Did forth issue, all ready for the fight:
On th' other side her foe appeared soone in sight.

XXVIII
But ere they reared hand, the Amazone
Began the streight conditions to propound,
With which she used still to tye her fone:
To serve her so, as she the rest had bound.
Which when the other heard, she sternly frownd
For high disdaine of such indignity,
And would no lenger treat, but bad them sound.
For her no other termes should ever tie,
Then what prescribed were by lawes of chevalrie.

XXIX
The trumpets sound, and they together run
With greedy rage, and with their faulchins smot;
Ne either sought the others strokes to shun,
But through great fury both their skill forgot,
And practicke use in armes: ne spared not
Their dainty parts, which Nature had created
So faire and tender, without staine or spot,
For other uses then they them translated;
Which they now hackt and hewd, as if such use they hated.

XXX
As when a tygre and a lionesse
Are met at spoyling of some hungry pray,
Both challenge it with equall greedinesse:
But first the tygre clawes thereon did lay;
And therefore loth to loose her right away,

Doth in defence thereof full stoutly stond:
To which the lion strongly doth gainesay,
That she to hunt the beast first tooke in hond;
And therefore ought it have, where ever she it fond.

XXXI
Full fiercely layde the Amazon about,
And dealt her blowes unmercifully sore:
Which Britomart withstood with courage stout,
And them repaide againe with double more.
So long they fought, that all the grassie flore
Was fild with bloud, which from their sides did flow,
And gushed through their armes, that all in gore
They trode, and on the ground their lives did strow,
Like fruitles seede, of which untimely death should grow.

XXXII
At last proud Radigund with fell despight,
Having by chaunce espide advantage neare,
Let drive at her with all her dreadfull might,
And thus upbrayding said: 'This token beare
Unto the man whom thou doest love so deare;
And tell him for his sake thy life thou gavest.'
Which spitefull words she sore engriev'd to heare,
Thus answer'd: 'Lewdly thou my love depravest,
Who shortly must repent that now so vainely bravest.'

XXXIII
Nath'lesse that stroke so cruell passage found,
That, glauncing on her shoulder plate, it bit
Unto the bone, and made a griesly wound,
That she her shield through raging smart of it
Could scarse uphold; yet soone she it requit:
For having force increast through furious paine,
She her so rudely on the helmet smit,
That it empierced to the very braine,
And her proud person low prostrated on the plaine.

XXXIV
Where being layd, the wrothfull Britonesse
Stayd not till she came to her selfe againe,
But in revenge both of her loves distresse,
And her late vile reproch, though vaunted vaine,
And also of her wound, which sore did paine,
She with one stroke both head and helmet cleft.
Which dreadfull sight when all her warlike traine
There present saw, each one, of sence bereft,
Fled fast into the towne, and her sole victor left.

XXXV
But yet so fast they could not home retrate,

But that swift Talus did the formost win;
And pressing through the preace unto the gate,
Pelmell with them attonce did enter in.
There then a piteous slaughter did begin:
For all that ever came within his reach
He with his yron flale did thresh so thin,
That he no worke at all left for the leach:
Like to an hideous storme, which nothing may empeach.

XXXVI
And now by this the noble conqueresse
Her selfe came in, her glory to partake;
Where, though revengefull vow she did professe,
Yet when she saw the heapes which he did make
Of slaughtred carkasses, her heart did quake
For very ruth, which did it almost rive,
That she his fury willed him to slake:
For else he sure had left not one alive,
But all, in his revenge, of spirite would deprive.

XXXVII
Tho, when she had his execution stayd,
She for that yron prison did enquire,
In which her wretched love was captive layd:
Which breaking open with indignant ire,
She entred into all the partes entire:
Where when she saw that lothly uncouth sight,
Of men disguiz'd in womanishe attire,
Her heart gan grudge, for very deepe despight
Of so unmanly maske, in misery misdight.

XXXVIII
At last when as to her owne love she came,
Whom like disguize no lesse deformed had,
At sight thereof abasht with secrete shame,
She turnd her head aside, as nothing glad
To have beheld a spectacle so bad.
And then too well beleev'd that which tofore
Jealous suspect as true untruely drad:
Which vaine conceipt now nourishing no more,
She sought with ruth to salve his sad misfortunes sore.

XXXIX
Not so great wonder and astonishment
Did the most chast Penelope possesse,
To see her lord, that was reported drent,
And dead long since in dolorous distresse,
Come home to her in piteous wretchednesse,
After long travell of full twenty yeares,
That she knew not his favours likelynesse,
For many scarres and many hoary heares,

But stood long staring on him, mongst uncertaine feares.

XL
'Ah! my deare lord, what sight is this?' quoth she;
'What May-game hath misfortune made of you?
Where is that dreadfull manly looke? where be
Those mighty palmes, the which ye wont t' embrew
In bloud of kings, and great hoastes to subdew?
Could ought on earth so wondrous change have wrought,
As to have robde you of that manly hew?
Could so great courage stouped have to ought?
Then farewell, fleshly force; I see thy pride is nought.'

XLI
Thenceforth she streight into a bowre him brought,
And causd him those uncomely weedes undight,
And in their steede for other rayment sought,
Whereof there was great store, and armors bright,
Which had bene reft from many a noble knight;
Whom that proud Amazon subdewed had,
Whilest fortune favourd her successe in fight:
In which when as she him anew had clad,
She was reviv'd, and joyd much in his semblance glad.

XLII
So there a while they afterwards remained,
Him to refresh, and her late wounds to heale:
During which space she there as princes rained,
And changing all that forme of common weale,
The liberty of women did repeale,
Which they had long usurpt; and them restoring
To mens subjection, did true justice deale:
That all they, as a goddesse her adoring,
Her wisedome did admire, and hearkned to her loring.

XLIII
For all those knights, which long in captive shade
Had shrowded bene, she did from thraldome free,
And magistrates of all that city made,
And gave to them great living and large fee:
And that they should for ever faithfull bee,
Made them sweare fealty to Artegall:
Who when him selfe now well recur'd did see,
He purposd to proceed, what so be fall,
Uppon his first adventure, which him forth did call.

XLIV
Full sad and sorrowfull was Britomart
For his departure, her new cause of griefe;
Yet wisely moderated her owne smart,
Seeing his honor, which she tendred chiefe,

Consisted much in that adventures priefe.
The care whereof, and hope of his successe,
Gave unto her great comfort and reliefe,
That womanish complaints she did represse,
And tempred for the time her present heavinesse.

XLV
There she continu'd for a certaine space,
Till through his want her woe did more increase:
Then, hoping that the change of aire and place
Would change her paine, and sorrow somewhat ease,
She parted thence, her anguish to appease.
Meane while her noble lord, Sir Artegall,
Went on his way, ne ever howre did cease,
Till he redeemed had that lady thrall:
That for another canto will more fitly fall.

CANTO VIII

Prince Arthure and Sir Artegall
Free Samient from feare:
They slay the Soudan, drive his wife
Adicia to despaire.

I
Nought under heaven so strongly doth allure
The sence of man, and all his minde possesse,
As beauties lovely baite, that doth procure
Great warriours oft their rigour to represse,
And mighty hands forget their manlinesse;
Drawne with the powre of an heart-robbing eye,
And wrapt in fetters of a golden tresse,
That can with melting pleasaunce mollifye
Their hardned hearts, enur'd to bloud and cruelty.

II
So whylome learnd that mighty Jewish swaine,
Each of whose lockes did match a man in might,
To lay his spoiles before his lemans traine:
So also did that great Oetean knight
For his loves sake his lions skin undight:
And so did warlike Antony neglect
The worlds whole rule for Cleopatras sight.
Such wondrous powre hath wemens faire aspect,
To captive men, and make them all the world reject.

III

Yet could it not sterne Artegall retaine,
Nor hold from suite of his avowed quest,
Which he had undertane to Gloriane;
But left his love, albe her strong request,
Faire Britomart, in languor and unrest,
And rode him selfe uppon his first intent:
Ne day nor night did ever idly rest;
Ne wight but onely Talus with him went,
The true guide of his way and vertuous government.

IV

So travelling, he chaunst far off to heed
A damzell, flying on a palfrey fast
Before two knights, that after her did speed
With all their powre, and her full fiercely chast
In hope to have her overhent at last:
Yet fled she fast, and both them farre outwent,
Carried with wings of feare, like fowle aghast,
With locks all loose, and rayment all torent;
And ever as she rode, her eye was backeward bent.

V

Soone after these he saw another knight,
That after those two former rode apace,
With speare in rest, and prickt with all his might:
So ran they all, as they had bene at bace,
They being chased, that did others chase.
At length he saw the hindmost overtake
One of those two, and force him turne his face;
How ever loth he were his way to slake,
Yet mote he algates now abide, and answere make.

VI

But th' other still pursu'd the fearefull mayd;
Who still from him as fast away did flie,
Ne once for ought her speedy passage stayd,
Till that at length she did before her spie
Sir Artegall, to whom she streight did hie
With gladfull hast, in hope of him to get
Succour against her greedy enimy:
Who, seeing her approch, gan forward set,
To save her from her feare, and him from force to let.

VII

But he like hound full greedy of his pray,
Being impatient of impediment,
Continu'd still his course, and by the way
Thought with his speare him quight have overwent.
So both together, ylike felly bent,
Like fiercely met. But Artegall was stronger,
And better skild in tilt and turnament,

And bore him quite out of his saddle, longer
Then two speares length: so mischiefe overmatcht the wronger.

VIII
And in his fall misfortune him mistooke;
For on his head unhappily he pight,
That his owne waight his necke asunder broke,
And left there dead. Meane while the other knight
Defeated had the other faytour quight,
And all his bowels in his body brast:
Whom leaving there in that dispiteous plight,
He ran still on, thinking to follow fast
His other fellow Pagan, which before him past.

IX
In stead of whom finding there ready prest
Sir Artegall, without discretion
He at him ran, with ready speare in rest:
Who, seeing him come still so fiercely on,
Against him made againe. So both anon
Together met, and strongly either strooke
And broke their speares; yet neither has forgon
His horses backe, yet to and fro long shooke,
And tottred like two towres, which through a tempest quooke.

X
But when againe they had recovered sence,
They drew their swords, in mind to make amends
For what their speares had fayld of their pretence.
Which when the damzell, who those deadly ends
Of both her foes had seene, and now her frends
For her beginning a more fearefull fray,
She to them runnes in hast, and her haire rends,
Crying to them their cruell hands to stay,
Untill they both doe heare what she to them will say.

XI
They stayd their hands, when she thus gan to speake:
'Ah! gentle knights, what meane ye thus unwise
Upon your selves anothers wrong to wreake?
I am the wrong'd, whom ye did enterprise
Both to redresse, and both redrest likewise:
Witnesse the Paynims both, whom ye may see
There dead on ground. What doe ye then devise
Of more revenge? if more, then I am shee
Which was the roote of all; end your revenge on mee.'

XII
Whom when they heard so say, they lookt about,
To weete if it were true, as she had told;
Where when they saw their foes dead out of doubt,

Eftsoones they gan their wrothfull hands to hold,
And ventailes reare, each other to behold.
Tho, when as Artegall did Arthure vew,
So faire a creature, and so wondrous bold,
He much admired both his heart and hew,
And touched with intire affection, nigh him drew,

XIII
Saying: 'Sir knight, of pardon I you pray,
That all unweeting have you wrong'd thus sore,
Suffring my hand against my heart to stray:
Which if ye please forgive, I will therefore
Yeeld for amends my selfe yours evermore,
Or what so penaunce shall by you be red.'
To whom the Prince: 'Certes, me needeth more
To crave the same, whom errour so misled,
As that I did mistake the living for the ded.

XIV
'But sith ye please that both our blames shall die,
Amends may for the trespasse soone be made,
Since neither is endamadg'd much thereby.'
So can they both them selves full eath perswade
To faire accordaunce, and both faults to shade,
Either embracing other lovingly,
And swearing faith to either on his blade,
Never thenceforth to nourish enmity,
But either others cause to maintaine mutually.

XV
Then Artegall gan of the Prince enquire,
What were those knights, which there on ground were layd,
And had receiv'd their follies worthy hire,
And for what cause they chased so that mayd.
'Certes, I wote not well,' the Prince then sayd,
'But by adventure found them faring so,
As by the way unweetingly I strayd,
And lo the damzell selfe, whence all did grow,
Of whom we may at will the whole occasion know.'

XVI
Then they that damzell called to them nie,
And asked her, what were those two her fone,
From whom she earst so fast away did flie;
And what was she her selfe so woe begone,
And for what cause pursu'd of them attone.
To whom she thus: 'Then wote ye well, that I
Doe serve a queene, that not far hence doth wone,
A princesse of great powre and majestie,
Famous through all the world, and honor'd far and nie.

XVII
'Her name Mercilla most men use to call;
That is a mayden queene of high renowne,
For her great bounty knowen over all,
And soveraine grace, with which her royall crowne
She doth support, and strongly beateth downe
The malice of her foes, which her envy,
And at her happinesse do fret and frowne:
Yet she her selfe the more doth magnify,
And even to her foes her mercies multiply.

XVIII
'Mongst many which maligne her happy state,
There is a mighty man, which wonnes here by,
That with most fell despight and deadly hate
Seekes to subvert her crowne and dignity,
And all his powre doth thereunto apply:
And her good knights, of which so brave a band
Serves her as any princesse under sky,
He either spoiles, if they against him stand,
Or to his part allures, and bribeth under hand.

XIX
'Ne him sufficeth all the wrong and ill,
Which he unto her people does each day,
But that he seekes by traytrous traines to spill
Her person, and her sacred selfe to slay:
That, O ye heavens, defend, and turne away
From her unto the miscreant him selfe,
That neither hath religion nor fay,
But makes his god of his ungodly pelfe,
And idols serves; so let his idols serve the elfe.

XX
'To all which cruell tyranny, they say,
He is provokt, and stird up day and night
By his bad wife, that hight Adicia,
Who counsels him, through confidence of might,
To breake all bonds of law and rules of right.
For she her selfe professeth mortall foe
To Justice, and against her still doth fight,
Working to all that love her deadly woe,
And making all her knights and people to doe so.

XXI
'Which my liege lady seeing, thought it best,
With that his wife in friendly wise to deale,
For stint of strife and stablishment of rest
Both to her selfe and to her common weale,
And all forepast displeasures to repeale.
So me in message unto her she sent,

To treat with her, by way of enterdeale,
Of finall peace and faire attonement,
Which might concluded be by mutuall consent.

XXII
'All times have wont safe passage to afford
To messengers that come for causes just:
But this proude dame, disdayning all accord,
Not onely into bitter termes forth brust,
Reviling me, and rayling as she lust,
But lastly, to make proofe of utmost shame,
Me like a dog she out of dores did thrust,
Miscalling me by many a bitter name,
That never did her ill, ne once deserved blame.

XXIII
'And lastly, that no shame might wanting be,
When I was gone, soone after me she sent
These two false knights, whom there ye lying see,
To be by them dishonoured and shent:
But thankt be God, and your good hardiment,
They have the price of their owne folly payd.'
So said this damzell, that hight Samient,
And to those knights, for their so noble ayd,
Her selfe most gratefull shew'd, and heaped thanks repayd.

XXIV
But they now having throughly heard, and seene
Al those great wrongs, the which that mayd complained
To have bene done against her lady queene
By that proud dame, which her so much disdained,
Were moved much thereat, and twixt them fained
With all their force to worke avengement strong
Uppon the Souldan selfe, which it mayntained,
And on his lady, th' author of that wrong,
And uppon all those knights that did to her belong.

XXV
But thinking best by counterfet disguise
To their deseigne to make the easier way,
They did this complot twixt them selves devise:
First, that Sir Artegall should him array
Like one of those two knights which dead there lay;
And then that damzell, the sad Samient,
Should as his purchast prize with him convay
Unto the Souldans court, her to present
Unto his scornefull lady, that for her had sent.

XXVI
So as they had deviz'd, Sir Artegall
Him clad in th' armour of a Pagan knight,

And taking with him, as his vanquisht thrall,
That damzell, led her to the Souldans right.
Where soone as his proud wife of her had sight,
Forth of her window as she looking lay,
She weened streight it was her Paynim knight,
Which brought that damzell as his purchast pray;
And sent to him a page, that mote direct his way.

XXVII
Who bringing them to their appointed place,
Offred his service to disarme the knight;
But he refusing him to let unlace,
For doubt to be discovered by his sight,
Kept himselfe still in his straunge armour dight.
Soone after whom the Prince arrived there,
And sending to the Souldan in despight
A bold defyance, did of him requere
That damzell, whom he held as wrongfull prisonere.

XXVIII
Wherewith the Souldan all with furie fraught,
Swearing and banning most blasphemously,
Commaunded straight his armour to be brought,
And mounting straight upon a charret hye,
(With yron wheeles and hookes arm'd dreadfully,
And drawne of cruell steedes, which he had fed
With flesh of men, whom through fell tyranny
He slaughtred had, and ere they were halfe ded,
Their bodies to his beasts for provender did spred,)

XXIX
So forth he came, all in a cote of plate,
Burnisht with bloudie rust; whiles on the greene
The Briton Prince him readie did awayte,
In glistering armes right goodly well beseene,
That shone as bright as doth the heaven sheene;
And by his stirrup Talus did attend,
Playing his pages part, as he had beene
Before directed by his lord; to th' end
He should his flale to finall execution bend.

XXX
Thus goe they both together to their geare,
With like fieroe minds, but meanings different:
For the proud Souldan, with presumpteous cheare,
And countenance sublime and insolent,
Sought onely slaughter and avengement:
But the brave Prince for honour and for right,
Gainst tortious powre and lawlesse regiment,
In the behalfe of wronged weake did fight:
More in his causes truth he trusted then in might.

XXXI
Like to the Thracian tyrant, who, they say,
Unto his horses gave his guests for meat,
Till he himselfe was made their greedie pray,
And torne in peeces by Alcides great:
So thought the Souldan in his follies threat,
Either the Prince in peeces to have torne
With his sharpe wheeles, in his first rages heat,
Or under his fierce horses feet have borne,
And trampled downe in dust his thoughts disdained scorne.

XXXII
But the bold child that perill well espying,
If he too rashly to his charet drew,
Gave way unto his horses speedie flying,
And their resistlesse rigour did eschew.
Yet, as he passed by, the Pagan threw
A shivering dart with so impetuous force,
That, had he not it shun'd with heedfull vew,
It had himselfe transfixed, or his horse,
Or made them both one masse withouten more remorse.

XXXIII
Oft drew the Prince unto his charret nigh,
In hope some stroke to fasten on him neare;
But he was mounted in his seat so high,
And his wingfooted coursers him did beare
So fast away, that ere his readie speare
He could advance, he farre was gone and past.
Yet still he him did follow every where,
And followed was of him likewise full fast,
So long as in his steedes the flaming breath did last.

XXXIV
Againe the Pagan threw another dart,
Of which he had with him abundant store,
On every side of his embatteld cart,
And of all other weapons lesse or more,
Which warlike uses had deviz'd of yore.
The wicked shaft, guyded through th' ayrie wyde
By some bad spirit, that it to mischiefe bore,
Stayd not, till through his curat it did glyde,
And made a griesly wound in his enriven side.

XXXV
Much was he grieved with that haplesse throe,
That opened had the welspring of his blood;
But much the more that to his hatefull foe
He mote not come, to wreake his wrathfull mood.
That made him rave, like to a lyon wood,

Which, being wounded of the huntsmans hand,
Can not come neare him in the covert wood,
Where he with boughes hath built his shady stand,
And fenst himselfe about with many a flaming brand.

XXXVI
Still when he sought t' approch unto him ny,
His charret wheeles about him whirled round,
And made him backe againe as fast to fly;
And eke his steedes, like to an hungry hound,
That hunting after game hath carrion found,
So cruelly did him pursew and chace,
That his good steed, all were he much renound
For noble courage and for hardie race,
Durst not endure their sight, but fled from place to place.

XXXVII
Thus long they trast and traverst to and fro,
Seeking by every way to make some breach,
Yet could the Prince not nigh unto him goe,
That one sure stroke he might unto him reach,
Whereby his strengthes assay he might him teach.
At last from his victorious shield he drew
The vaile which did his powrefull light empeach;
And comming full before his horses vew,
As they upon him prest, it plaine to them did shew.

XXXVIII
Like lightening flash, that hath the gazer burned,
So did the sight thereof their sense dismay,
That backe againe upon themselves they turned,
And with their ryder ranne perforce away:
Ne could the Souldan them from flying stay
With raynes, or wonted rule, as well he knew.
Nought feared they what he could do or say,
But th' onely feare that was before their vew;
From which, like mazed deare, dismayfully they flew.

XXXIX
Fast did they fly as them their feete could beare,
High over hilles, and lowly over dales,
As they were follow'd of their former feare.
In vaine the Pagan bannes, and sweares, and rayles,
And backe with both his hands unto him hayles
The resty raynes, regarded now no more:
He to them calles and speakes, yet nought avayles;
They heare him not, they have forgot his lore,
But go which way they list; their guide they have forlore.

XL
As when the firie-mouthed steeds, which drew

The sunnes bright wayne to Phaetons decay,
Soone as they did the monstrous Scorpion vew,
With ugly craples crawling in their way,
The dreadfull sight did them so sore affray,
That their well knowen courses they forwent,
And leading th' ever-burning lampe astray,
This lower world nigh all to ashes brent,
And left their scorched path yet in the firmament.

XLI
Such was the furie of these head-strong steeds,
Soone as the infants sunlike shield they saw,
That all obedience both to words and deeds
They quite forgot, and scornd all former law:
Through woods, and rocks, and mountaines they did draw
The yron charet, and the wheeles did teare,
And tost the Paynim, without feare or awe;
From side to side they tost him here and there,
Crying to them in vaine, that nould his crying heare.

XLII
Yet still the Prince pursew'd him close behind,
Oft making offer him to smite, but found
No easie meanes according to his mind.
At last they have all overthrowne to ground,
Quite topside turvey, and the Pagan hound
Amongst the yron hookes and graples keene
Torne all to rags, and rent with many a wound,
That no whole peece of him was to be seene,
But scattred all about, and strow'd upon the greene.

XLIII
Like as the cursed sonne of Theseus,
That, following his chace in dewy morne,
To fly his stepdames loves outrageous,
Of his owne steedes was all to peeces torne,
And his faire limbs left in the woods forlorne;
That for his sake Diana did lament,
And all the wooddy nymphes did wayle and mourne:
So was this Souldan rapt and all to-rent,
That of his shape appear'd no litle moniment.

XLIV
Onely his shield and armour, which there lay,
Though nothing whole, but all to-brusd and broken,
He up did take, and with him brought away,
That mote remaine for an eternall token
To all mongst whom this storie should be spoken,
How worthily, by Heavens high decree,
Justice that day of wrong her selfe had wroken,
That all men which that spectacle did see,

By like ensample mote for ever warned bee.

XLV
So on a tree, before the tyrants dore,
He caused them be hung in all mens sight,
To be a moniment for evermore.
Which when his ladie from the castles hight
Beheld, it much appald her troubled spright:
Yet not, as women wont, in dolefull fit
She was dismayd, or faynted through affright,
But gathered unto her her troubled wit,
And gan eftsoones devize to be aveng'd for it.

XLVI
Streight downe she ranne, like an enraged cow,
That is berobbed of her youngling dere,
With knife in hand, and fatally did vow
To wreake her on that mayden messengere,
Whom she had causd be kept as prisonere
By Artegall, misween'd for her owne knight,
That brought her backe. And comming present there,
She at her ran with all her force and might,
All flaming with revenge and furious despight.

XLVII
Like raging Ino, when with knife in hand
She threw her husbands murdred infant out;
Or fell Medea, when on Colchicke strand
Her brothers bones she scattered all about;
Or as that madding mother, mongst the rout
Of Bacchus priests, her owne deare flesh did teare.
Yet neither Ino, nor Medea stout,
Nor all the Mœnades so furious were,
As this bold woman, when she saw that damzell there.

XLVIII
But Artegall, being thereof aware,
Did stay her cruell hand, ere she her raught,
And as she did her selfe to strike prepare,
Out of her fist the wicked weapon caught:
With that, like one enfelon'd or distraught,
She forth did rome, whether her rage her bore,
With franticke passion and with furie fraught;
And breaking forth out at a posterne dore,
Unto the wyld ranne, her dolours to deplore.

XLIX
As a mad bytch, when as the franticke fit
Her burning tongue with rage inflamed hath,
Doth runne at randon, and with furious bit
Snatching at every thing, doth wreake her wrath

On man and beast that commeth in her path.
There they doe say that she transformed was
Into a tygre, and that tygres scath
In crueltie and outrage she did pas,
To prove her surname true, that she imposed has.

L
Then Artegall himselfe discovering plaine,
Did issue forth gainst all that warlike rout
Of knights and armed men, which did maintaine
That ladies part, and to the Souldan lout:
All which he did assault with courage stout,
All were they nigh an hundred knights of name,
And like wyld goates them chaced all about,
Flying from place to place with cowheard shame,
So that with finall force them all he overcame.

LI
Then caused he the gates be opened wyde,
And there the Prince, as victour of that day,
With tryumph entertayn'd and glorifyde,
Presenting him with all the rich array
And roiall pompe, which there long hidden lay,
Purchast through lawlesse powre and tortious wrong
Of that proud Souldan, whom he earst did slay.
So both, for rest there having stayd not long,
Marcht with that mayd, fit matter for another song.

CANTO IX

Arthur and Artegall catch Guyle,
Whom Talus doth dismay:
They to Mercillaes pallace come,
And see her rich array.

I
What tygre, or what other salvage wight,
Is so exceeding furious and fell
As Wrong, when it hath arm'd it selfe with might?
Not fit mongst men, that doe with reason mell,
But mongst wyld beasts and salvage woods to dwell;
Where still the stronger doth the weake devoure,
And they that most in boldnesse doe excell
Are dreadded most, and feared for their powre;
Fit for Adicia, there to build her wicked bowre.

II

There let her wonne farre from resort of men,
Where righteous Artegall her late exyled;
There let her ever keepe her damned den,
Where none may be with her lewd parts defyled,
Nor none but beasts may be of her despoyled:
And turne we to the noble Prince, where late
We did him leave, after that he had foyled
The cruell Souldan, and with dreadfull fate
Had utterly subverted his unrighteous state.

III
Where having with Sir Artegall a space
Well solast in that Souldans late delight,
They both resolving now to leave the place,
Both it and all the wealth therein behight
Unto that damzell in her ladies right,
And so would have departed on their way.
But she them woo'd by all the meanes she might,
And earnestly besought, to wend that day
With her, to see her ladie thence not farre away.

IV
By whose entreatie both they overcommen,
Agree to goe with her, and by the way,
(As often falles) of sundry things did commen.
Mongst which that damzell did to them bewray
A straunge adventure, which not farre thence lay;
To weet, a wicked villaine, bold and stout,
Which wonned in a rocke not farre away,
That robbed all the countrie there about,
And brought the pillage home, whence none could get it out.

V
Thereto both his owne wylie wit (she sayd)
And eke the fastnesse of his dwelling place,
Both unassaylable, gave him great ayde:
For he so crafty was to forge and face,
So light of hand, and nymble of his pace,
So smooth of tongue, and subtile in his tale,
That could deceive one looking in his face;
Therefore by name Malengin they him call,
Well knowen by his feates, and famous over all.

VI
Through these his slights he many doth confound,
And eke the rocke, in which he wonts to dwell,
Is wondrous strong, and hewen farre under ground
A dreadfull depth, how deepe no man can tell;
But some doe say, it goeth downe to hell.
And all within, it full of wyndings is,
And hidden wayes, that scarse an hound by smell

Can follow out those false footsteps of his,
Ne none can backe returne that once are gone amis.

VII
Which when those knights had heard, their harts gan earne
To understand that villeins dwelling place,
And greatly it desir'd of her to learne,
And by which way they towards it should trace.
'Were not,' sayd she, 'that it should let your pace
Towards my ladies presence by you ment,
I would you guyde directly to the place.'
'Then let not that,' said they, 'stay your intent;
For neither will one foot, till we that carle have hent.'

VIII
So forth they past, till they approched ny
Unto the rocke where was the villains won:
Which when the damzell neare at hand did spy,
She warn'd the knights thereof: who thereupon
Gan to advize what best were to be done.
So both agreed to send that mayd afore,
Where she might sit nigh to the den alone,
Wayling, and raysing pittifull uprore,
As if she did some great calamitie deplore.

IX
With noyse whereof when as the caytive carle
Should issue forth, in hope to find some spoyle,
They in awayt would closely him ensnarle,
Ere to his den he backward could recoyle,
And so would hope him easily to foyle.
The damzell straight went, as she was directed,
Unto the rocke, and there upon the soyle
Having her selfe in wretched wize abjected,
Gan weepe and wayle, as if great griefe had her affected.

X
The cry whereof entring the hollow cave,
Eftsoones brought forth the villaine, as they ment,
With hope of her some wishfull boot to have.
Full dreadfull wight he was, as ever went
Upon the earth, with hollow eyes deepe pent,
And long curld locks, that downe his shoulders shagged,
And on his backe an uncouth vestiment
Made of straunge stuffe, but all to-worne and ragged,
And underneath his breech was all to-torne and jagged.

XI
And in his hand an huge long staffe he held,
Whose top was arm'd with many an yron hooke,
Fit to catch hold of all that he could weld,

Or in the compasse of his clouches tooke;
And ever round about he cast his looke.
Als at his backe a great wyde net he bore,
With which he seldome fished at the brooke,
But usd to fish for fooles on the dry shore,
Of which he in faire weather wont to take great store.

XII
Him when the damzell saw fast by her side,
So ugly creature, she was nigh dismayd,
And now for helpe aloud in earnest cride.
But when the villaine saw her so affrayd,
He gan with guilefull words her to perswade
To banish feare, and with Sardonian smyle
Laughing on her, his false intent to shade,
Gan forth to lay his bayte her to beguyle,
That from her self unwares he might her steale the whyle.

XIII
Like as the fouler on his guilefull pype
Charmes to the birds full many a pleasant lay,
That they the whiles may take lesse heedie keepe,
How he his nets doth for their ruine lay:
So did the villaine to her prate and play,
And many pleasant trickes before her show,
To turne her eyes from his intent away:
For he in slights and jugling feates did flow,
And of legierdemayne the mysteries did know.

XIV
To which whilest she lent her intentive mind,
He suddenly his net upon her threw,
That oversprad her like a puffe of wind;
And snatching her soone up, ere well she knew,
Ran with her fast away unto his mew,
Crying for helpe aloud. But when as ny
He came unto his cave, and there did vew
The armed knights stopping his passage by,
He threw his burden downe, and fast away did fly.

XV
But Artegall him after did pursew,
The whiles the Prince there kept the entrance still:
Up to the rocke he ran, and thereon flew
Like a wyld gote, leaping from hill to hill,
And dauncing on the craggy cliffes at will;
That deadly daunger seem'd in all mens sight,
To tempt such steps, where footing was so ill:
Ne ought avayled for the armed knight
To thinke to follow him, that was so swift and light.

XVI
Which when he saw, his yron man he sent
To follow him; for he was swift in chace.
He him pursewd, where ever that he went;
Both over rockes, and hilles, and every place,
Where so he fled, he followd him apace:
So that he shortly forst him to forsake
The hight, and downe descend unto the base.
There he him courst a fresh, and soone did make
To leave his proper forme, and other shape to take.

XVII
Into a foxe himselfe he first did tourne;
But he him hunted like a foxe full fast:
Then to a bush himselfe he did transforme;
But he the bush did beat, till that at last
Into a bird it chaung'd, and from him past,
Flying from tree to tree, from wand to wand:
But he then stones at it so long did cast,
That like a stone it fell upon the land;
But he then tooke it up, and held fast in his hand.

XVIII
So he it brought with him unto the knights,
And to his lord, Sir Artegall, it lent,
Warning him hold it fast, for feare of slights.
Who whilest in hand it gryping hard he hent,
Into a hedgehogge all unwares it went,
And prickt him so that he away it threw.
Then gan it runne away incontinent,
Being returned to his former hew:
But Talus soone him overtooke, and backward drew.

XIX
But when as he would to a snake againe
Have turn'd himselfe, he with his yron flayle
Gan drive at him, with so huge might and maine,
That all his bones as small as sandy grayle
He broke, and did his bowels disentrayle;
Crying in vaine for helpe, when helpe was past.
So did deceipt the selfe deceiver fayle.
There they him left a carrion outcast,
For beasts and foules to feede upon for their repast.

XX
Thence forth they passed with that gentle mayd,
To see her ladie, as they did agree.
To which when she approched, thus she sayd:
'Loe now, right noble knights, arriv'd ye bee
Nigh to the place which ye desir'd to see:
There shall ye see my soverayne Lady Queene,

Most sacred wight, most debonayre and free,
That ever yet upon this earth was seene,
Or that with diademe hath ever crowned beene.'

XXI
The gentle knights rejoyced much to heare
The prayses of that prince so manifold,
And passing litle further, commen were
Where they a stately pallace did behold,
Of pompous show, much more then she had told;
With many towres and tarras mounted hye,
And all their tops bright glistering with gold,
That seemed to outshine the dimmed skye,
And with their brightnesse daz'd the straunge beholders eye.

XXII
There they alighting, by that damzell were
Directed in, and shewed all the sight:
Whose porch, that most magnificke did appeare,
Stood open wyde to all men day and night;
Yet warded well by one of mickle might,
That sate thereby, with gyantlike resemblance,
To keepe out Guyle, and Malice, and Despight,
That under shew oftimes of fayned semblance
Are wont in princes courts to worke great scath and hindrance.

XXIII
His name was Awe; by whom they passing in
Went up the hall, that was a large wyde roome,
All full of people making troublous din,
And wondrous noyse, as if that there were some
Which unto them was dealing righteous doome.
By whom they passing, through the thickest preasse,
The marshall of the hall to them did come;
His name hight Order, who, commaunding peace,
Them guyded through the throng, that did their clamors ceasse.

XXIV
They ceast their clamors upon them to gaze;
Whom seeing all in armour bright as day,
Straunge there to see, it did them much amaze,
And with unwonted terror halfe affray:
For never saw they there the like array;
Ne ever was the name of warre there spoken,
But joyous peace and quietnesse alway,
Dealing just judgements, that mote not be broken
For any brybes, or threates of any to be wroken.

XXV
There as they entred at the scriene, they saw
Some one, whose tongue was for his trespasse vyle

Nayld to a post, adjudged so by law:
For that therewith he falsely did revyle
And foule blaspheme that queene for forged guyle,
Both with bold speaches which he blazed had,
And with lewd poems which he did compyle;
For the bold title of a poet bad
He on himselfe had ta'en, and rayling rymes had sprad.

XXVI
Thus there he stood, whylest high over his head
There written was the purport of his sin,
In cyphers strange, that few could rightly read,
Bon font: but Bon, that once had written bin,
Was raced out, and Mal was now put in:
So now Malfont was plainely to be red;
Eyther for th' evill which he did therein,
Or that he likened was to a welhed
Of evill words, and wicked sclaunders by him shed.

XXVII
They, passing by, were guyded by degree
Unto the presence of that gratious queene:
Who sate on high, that she might all men see,
And might of all men royally be seene,
Upon a throne of gold full bright and sheene,
Adorned all with gemmes of endlesse price,
As either might for wealth have gotten bene,
Or could be fram'd by workmans rare device;
And all embost with lyons and with flourdelice.

XXVIII
All over her a cloth of state was spred,
Not of rich tissew, nor of cloth of gold,
Nor of ought else that may be richest red,
But like a cloud, as likest may be told,
That her brode spreading wings did wyde unfold;
Whose skirts were bordred with bright sunny beams,
Glistring like gold, amongst the plights enrold,
And here and there shooting forth silver streames,
Mongst which crept litle angels through the glittering gleames.

XXIX
Seemed those litle angels did uphold
The cloth of state, and on their purpled wings
Did beare the pendants, through their nimblesse bold:
Besides, a thousand more of such as sings
Hymnes to High God, and carols heavenly things,
Encompassed the throne on which she sate:
She angel-like, the heyre of ancient kings
And mightie conquerors, in royall state,
Whylest kings and kesars at her feet did them prostrate.

XXX

Thus she did sit in soverayne majestie,
Holding a scepter in her royall hand,
The sacred pledge of peace and clemencie,
With which High God had blest her happie land,
Maugre so many foes which did withstand.
But at her feet her sword was likewise layde,
Whose long rest rusted the bright steely brand;
Yet when as foes enforst, or friends sought ayde,
She could it sternely draw, that all the world dismayde.

XXXI

And round about, before her feet there sate
A bevie of faire virgins clad in white,
That goodly seem'd t' adorne her royall state,
All lovely daughters of high Jove, that hight
Litæ, by him begot in loves delight
Upon the righteous Themis: those they say
Upon Joves judgement seat wayt day and night,
And when in wrath he threats the worlds decay,
They doe his anger calme, and cruell vengeance stay.

XXXII

They also doe by his divine permission
Upon the thrones of mortall princes tend,
And often treat for pardon and remission
To suppliants, through frayltie which offend.
Those did upon Mercillaes throne attend:
Just Dice, wise Eunomie, myld Eirene;
And them amongst, her glorie to commend,
Sate goodly Temperance in garments clene,
And sacred Reverence, yborne of heavenly strene.

XXXIII

Thus did she sit in royall rich estate,
Admyr'd of many, honoured of all,
An underneath her feete, there as she sate,
An huge great lyon lay, that mote appall
An hardie courage, like captived thrall,
With a strong yron chaine and coller bound,
That once he could not move, nor quich at all;
Yet did he murmure with rebellious sound,
And softly royne, when salvage choler gan redound.

XXXIV

So sitting high in dreaded soverayntie,
Those two strange knights were to her presence brought;
Who, bowing low before her majestie,
Did to her myld obeysance, as they ought,
And meekest boone that they imagine mought.

To whom she eke inclyning her withall,
As a faire stoupe of her high soaring thought,
A chearefull countenance on them let fall,
Yet tempred with some majestie imperiall.

XXXV
As the bright sunne, what time his fierie teme
Towards the westerne brim begins to draw,
Gins to abate the brightnesse of his beme,
And fervour of his flames somewhat adaw:
So did this mightie ladie, when she saw
Those two strange knights such homage to her make,
Bate somewhat of that majestie and awe,
That whylome wont to doe so many quake,
And with more myld aspect those two to entertake.

XXXVI
Now at that instant, as occasion fell,
When these two stranger knights arriv'd in place,
She was about affaires of common wele,
Dealing of justice with indifferent grace,
And hearing pleas of people meane and base.
Mongst which, as then, there was for to be heard
The tryall of a great and weightie case,
Which on both sides was then debating hard:
But at the sight of these, those were a while debard.

XXXVII
But after all her princely entertayne,
To th' hearing of that former cause in hand
Her selfe eftsoones she gan convert againe;
Which that those knights likewise mote understand,
And witnesse forth aright in forrain land,
Taking them up unto her stately throne,
Where they mote heare the matter throughly scand
On either part, she placed th' one on th' one,
The other on the other side, and neare them none.

XXXVIII
Then was there brought, as prisoner to the barre,
A ladie of great countenance and place,
But that she it with foule abuse did marre;
Yet did appeare rare beautie in her face,
But blotted with condition vile and base,
That all her other honour did obscure,
And titles of nobilitie deface:
Yet in that wretched semblant, she did sure
The peoples great compassion unto her allure.

XXXIX
Then up arose a person of deepe reach,

And rare in-sight, hard matters to revele;
That well could charme his tongue, and time his speach
To all assayes; his name was called Zele:
He gan that ladie strongly to appele
Of many haynous crymes, by her enured,
And with sharpe reasons rang her such a pele,
That those whom she to pitie had allured
He now t' abhorre and loath her person had procured.

XL
First gan he tell, how this, that seem'd so faire
And royally arayd, Duessa hight,
That false Duessa, which had wrought great care
And mickle mischiefe unto many a knight,
By her beguyled and confounded quight:
But not for those she now in question came,
Though also those mote question'd be aright,
But for vyld treasons and outrageous shame,
Which she against the dred Mercilla oft did frame.

XLI
For she whylome (as ye mote yet right well
Remember) had her counsels false conspyred
With faithlesse Blandamour and Paridell,
(Both two her paramours, both by her hyred,
And both with hope of shadowes vaine inspyred.)
And with them practiz'd, how for to depryve
Mercilla of her crowne, by her aspyred,
That she might it unto her selfe deryve,
And tryumph in their blood, whom she to death did dryve.

XLII
But through high heavens grace, which favour not
The wicked driftes of trayterous desynes
Gainst loiall princes, all this cursed plot,
Ere proofe it tooke, discovered was betymes,
And th' actours won the meede meet for their crymes.
Such be the meede of all that by such mene
Unto the type of kingdomes title clymes.
But false Duessa, now untitled queene,
Was brought to her sad doome, as here was to be seene.

XLIII
Strongly did Zele her haynous fact enforce,
And many other crimes of foule defame
Against her brought, to banish all remorse,
And aggravate the horror of her blame.
And with him to make part against her, came
Many grave persons, that against her pled:
First was a sage old syre, that had to name
The Kingdomes Care, with a white silver hed,

That many high regards and reasons gainst her red.

XLIV
Then gan Authority her to appose
With peremptorie powre, that made all mute;
And then the Law of Nations gainst her rose,
And reasons brought, that no man could refute;
Next gan Religion gainst her to impute
High Gods beheast, and powre of holy lawes;
Then gan the Peoples Cry and Commons Sute
Importune care of their owne publicke cause;
And lastly Justice charged her with breach of lawes.

XLV
But then for her, on the contrarie part,
Rose many advocates for her to plead:
First there came Pittie, with full tender hart,
And with her joyn'd Regard of Womanhead;
And then came Daunger, threatning hidden dread
And high alliance unto forren powre;
Then came Nobilitie of Birth, that bread
Great ruth through her misfortunes tragicke stowre;
And lastly Griefe did plead, and many teares forth powre.

XLVI
With the neare touch whereof in tender hart
The Briton Prince was sore empassionate,
And woxe inclined much unto her part,
Through the sad terror of so dreadfull fate,
And wretched ruine of so high estate,
That for great ruth his courage gan relent.
Which when as Zele perceived to abate,
He gan his earnest fervour to augment,
And many fearefull objects to them to present.

XLVII
He gan t' efforce the evidence anew,
And new accusements to produce in place:
He brought forth that old hag of hellish hew,
The cursed Ate, brought her face to face,
Who privie was, and partie in the case:
She, glad of spoyle and ruinous decay,
Did her appeach, and, to her more disgrace,
The plot of all her practise did display,
And all her traynes and all her treasons forth did lay.

XLVIII
Then brought he forth, with griesly grim aspect,
Abhorred Murder, who with bloudie knyfe
Yet dropping fresh in hand did her detect,
And there with guiltie bloudshed charged ryfe:

Then brought he forth Sedition, breeding stryfe
In troublous wits, and mutinous uprore:
Then brought he forth Incontinence of Lyfe,
Even foule Adulterie her face before,
And lewd Impietie, that her accused sore.

XLIX
All which when as the Prince had heard and seene,
His former fancies ruth he gan repent,
And from her partie eftsoones was drawen cleene.
But Artegall, with constant firme intent,
For zeale of justice was against her bent.
So was she guiltie deemed of them all.
Then Zele began to urge her punishment,
And to their queene for judgement loudly call,
Unto Mercilla myld, for justice gainst the thrall.

L
But she, whose princely breast was touched nere
With piteous ruth of her so wretched plight,
Though plaine she saw, by all that she did heare,
That she of death was guiltie found by right,
Yet would not let just vengeance on her light;
But rather let in stead thereof to fall
Few perling drops from her faire lampes of light;
The which she covering with her purple pall
Would have the passion hid, and up arose withall.

CANTO X

Prince Arthur takes the enterprize
For Belgee for to fight:
Gerioneos seneschall
He slayes in Belges right.

I
Some clarkes doe doubt in their devicefull art,
Whether this heavenly thing whereof I treat,
To weeten Mercie, be of Justice part,
Or drawne forth from her by divine extreate.
This well I wote, that sure she is as great,
And meriteth to have as high a place,
Sith in th' Almighties everlasting seat
She first was bred, and borne of heavenly race;
From thence pour'd down on men, by influence of grace.

II

For if that vertue be of so great might,
Which from just verdict will for nothing start,
But, to preserve inviolated right,
Oft spiles the principall, to save the part;
So much more then is that of powre and art,
That seekes to save the subject of her skill,
Yet never doth from doome of right depart:
As it is greater prayse to save then spill,
And better to reforme then to cut off the ill.

III
Who then can thee, Mercilla, throughly prayse,
That herein doest all earthly princess pas?
What heavenly muse shall thy great honour rayse
Up to the skies, whence first deriv'd it was,
And now on earth it selfe enlarged has
From th' utmost brinke of the Americke shore
Unto the margent of the Molucas?
Those nations farre thy justice doe adore:
But thine owne people do thy mercy prayse much more.

IV
Much more it praysed was of those two knights,
The noble Prince and righteous Artegall,
When they had seene and heard her doome a rights
Against Duessa, damned by them all;
But by her tempred without griefe or gall,
Till strong constraint did her thereto enforce:
And yet even then running her wilfull fall
With more then needfull naturall remorse,
And yeelding the last honour to her wretched corse.

V
During all which, those knights continu'd there,
Both doing and receiving curtesies
Of that great ladie, who with goodly chere
Them entertayn'd, fit for their dignities,
Approving dayly to their noble eyes
Royall examples of her mercies rare,
And worthie paterns of her clemencies;
Which till this day mongst many living are,
Who them to their posterities doe still declare.

VI
Amongst the rest, which in that space befell,
There came two springals of full tender yeares,
Farre thence from forrein land, where they did dwell,
To seeke for succour of her and of her peares,
With humble prayers and intreatfull teares;
Sent by their mother, who a widow was,
Wrapt in great dolours and in deadly feares

By a strong tyrant, who invaded has
Her land, and slaine her children ruefully, alas!

VII
Her name was Belgæ, who in former age
A ladie of great worth and wealth had beene,
And mother of a frutefull heritage,
Even seventeene goodly sonnes; which who had seene
In their first flowre, before this fatall teene
Them overtooke, and their faire blossomes blasted,
More happie mother would her surely weene
Then famous Niobe, before she tasted
Latonaes childrens wrath, that all her issue wasted.

VIII
But this fell tyrant, through his tortious powre,
Had left her now but five of all that brood:
For twelve of them he did by times devoure,
And to his idole sacrifice their blood,
Whylest he of none was stopped, nor withstood.
For soothly he was one of matchlesse might,
Of horrible aspect and dreadfull mood,
And had three bodies in one wast empight,
And th' armes and legs of three, to succour him in fight.

IX
And sooth they say that he was borne and bred
Of gyants race, the sonne of Geryon,
He that whylome in Spaine so sore was dred
For his huge powre and great oppression,
Which brought that land to his subjection
Through his three bodies powre, in one combynd;
And eke all strangers, in that region
Arryving, to his kyne for food assynd;
The fayrest kyne alive, but of the fiercest kynd.

X
For they were all, they say, of purple hew,
Kept by a cowheard, hight Eurytion,
A cruell carle, the which all strangers slew,
Ne day nor night did sleepe, t' attend them on,
But walkt about them ever and anone,
With his two headed dogge, that Orthrus hight;
Orthrus begotten by great Typhaon
And foule Echidna, in the house of Night;
But Hercules them all did overcome in fight.

XI
His sonne was this, Geryoneo hight;
Who, after that his monstrous father fell
Under Alcides club, streight tooke his flight

From that sad land, where he his syre did quell,
And came to this, where Belge then did dwell
And flourish in all wealth and happinesse,
Being then new made widow (as befell)
After her noble husbands late decesse;
Which gave beginning to her woe and wretchednesse.

XII
Then this bold tyrant, of her widowhed
Taking advantage, and her yet fresh woes,
Himselfe and service to her offered,
Her to defend against all forrein foes,
That should their powre against her right oppose.
Whereof she glad, now needing strong defence,
Him entertayn'd, and did her champion chose:
Which long he usd with carefull diligence,
The better to confirme her fearelesse confidence.

XIII
By meanes whereof, she did at last commit
All to his hands, and gave him soveraine powre
To doe what ever he thought good or fit.
Which having got, he gan forth from that howre
To stirre up strife, and many a tragicke stowre,
Giving her dearest children one by one
Unto a dreadfull monster to devoure,
And setting up an idole of his owne,
The image of his monstrous parent Geryone.

XIV
So tyrannizing, and oppressing all,
The woefull widow had no meanes now left,
But unto gratious great Mercilla call
For ayde against that cruell tyrants theft,
Ere all her children he from her had reft.
Therefore these two, her eldest sonnes, she sent,
To seeke for succour of this ladies gieft:
To whom their sute they humbly did present,
In th' hearing of full many knights and ladies gent.

XV
Amongst the which then fortuned to bee
The noble Briton Prince, with his brave peare;
Who when he none of all those knights did see
Hastily bent that enterprise to heare,
Nor undertake the same, for cowheard feare,
He stepped forth with courage bold and great,
Admyr'd of all the rest in presence there,
And humbly gan that mightie queene entreat
To graunt him that adventure for his former feat.

XVI
She gladly graunted it: then he straight way
Himselfe unto his journey gan prepare,
And all his armours readie dight that day,
That nought the morrow next mote stay his fare.
The morrow next appear'd, with purple hayre
Yet dropping fresh out of the Indian fount,
And bringing light into the heavens fayre,
When he was readie to his steede to mount,
Unto his way, which now was all his care and count.

XVII
Then taking humble leave of that great queene,
Who gave him roiall giftes and riches rare,
As tokens of her thankefull mind beseene,
And leaving Artegall to his owne care,
Upon his voyage forth he gan to fare,
With those two gentle youthes, which him did guide,
And all his way before him still prepare.
Ne after him did Artigall abide,
But on his first adventure forward forth did ride.

XVIII
It was not long till that the Prince arrived
Within the land where dwelt that ladie sad,
Whereof that tyrant had her now deprived,
And into moores and marshes banisht had,
Out of the pleasant soyle and citties glad,
In which she wont to harbour happily:
But now his cruelty so sore she drad,
That to those fennes for fastnesse she did fly,
And there her selfe did hyde from his hard tyranny.

XIX
There he her found in sorrow and dismay,
All solitarie without living wight;
For all her other children, through affray,
Had hid themselves, or taken further flight:
And eke her selfe through sudden strange affright,
When one in armes she saw, began to fly;
But when her owne two sonnes she had in sight,
She gan take hart, and looke up joyfully:
For well she wist this knight came succour to supply:

XX
And running unto them with greedy joyes,
Fell straight about their neckes, as they did kneele,
And bursting forth in teares, 'Ah! my sweet boyes,'
Sayd she, 'yet now I gin new life to feele,
And feeble spirits, that gan faint and reele,
Now rise againe at this your joyous sight.

Alreadie seemes that Fortunes headlong wheele
Begins to turne, and sunne to shine more bright
Then it was wont, through comfort of this noble knight.'

XXI
Then turning unto him, 'And you, sir knight,'
Said she, 'that taken have this toylesome paine
For wretched woman, miserable wight,
May you in heaven immortall guerdon gaine
For so great travell as you doe sustaine:
For other meede may hope for none of mee,
To whom nought else but bare life doth remaine;
And that so wretched one, as ye do see,
Is liker lingring death then loathed life to bee.'

XXII
Much was he moved with her piteous plight,
And low dismounting from his loftie steede,
Gan to recomfort her all that he might,
Seeking to drive away deepe rooted dreede,
With hope of helpe in that her greatest neede.
So thence he wished her with him to wend,
Unto some place where they mote rest and feede,
And she take comfort, which God now did send:
Good hart in evils doth the evils much amend.

XXIII
'Ay me!' sayd she, 'and whether shall I goe?
Are not all places full of forraine powres?
My pallaces possessed of my foe,
My cities sackt, and their sky-threating towres
Raced, and made smooth fields now full of flowres?
Onely these marishes and myrie bogs,
In which the fearefull ewftes do build their bowres,
Yeeld me an hostry mongst the croking frogs,
And harbour here in safety from those ravenous dogs.'

XXIV
'Nathlesse,' said he, 'deare ladie, with me goe;
Some place shall us receive, and harbour yield;
If not, we will it force, maugre your foe,
And purchase it to us with speare and shield:
And if all fayle, yet farewell open field:
The Earth to all her creatures lodging lends.'
With such his chearefull speaches he doth wield
Her mind so well, that to his will she bends,
And bynding up her locks and weeds, forth with him wends.

XXV
They came unto a citie farre up land,
The which whylome that ladies owne had bene;

But now by force extort out of her hand
By her strong foe, who had defaced cleene
Her stately towres and buildings sunny sheene,
Shut up her haven, mard her marchants trade,
Robbed her people, that full rich had beene,
And in her necke a castle huge had made,
The which did her commaund, without needing perswade.

XXVI
That castle was the strength of all that state,
Untill that state by strength was pulled downe,
And that same citie, so now ruinate,
Had bene the keye of all that kingdomes crowne;
Both goodly castle, and both goodly towne,
Till that th' offended Heavens list to lowre
Upon their blisse, and balefull Fortune frowne.
When those gainst states and kingdomes do conjure,
Who then can thinke their hedlong ruine to recure?

XXVII
But he had brought it now in servile bond,
And made it beare the yoke of Inquisition,
Stryving long time in vaine it to withstond;
Yet glad at last to make most base submission,
And life enjoy for any composition.
So now he hath new lawes and orders new
Imposd on it, with many a hard condition,
And forced it the honour that is dew
To God to doe unto his idole most untrew.

XXVIII
To him he hath, before this castle greene,
Built a faire chappell, and an altar framed
Of costly ivory, full rich beseene,
On which that cursed idole, farre proclamed,
He hath set up, and him his god hath named,
Offring to him in sinfull sacrifice
The flesh of men, to Gods owne likenesse framed,
And powring forth their bloud in brutishe wize,
That any yron eyes to see it would agrize.

XXIX
And for more horror and more crueltie,
Under that cursed idols altar stone
An hideous monster doth in darknesse lie,
Whose dreadfull shape was never seene of none
That lives on earth, but unto those alone
The which unto him sacrificed bee.
Those he devoures, they say, both flesh and bone:
What else they have is all the tyrants fee;
So that no whit of them remayning one may see.

XXX

There eke he placed a strong garrisone,
And set a seneschall of dreaded might,
That by his powre oppressed every one,
And vanquished all ventrous knights in fight;
To whom he wont shew all the shame he might,
After that them in battell he had wonne.
To which when now they gan approch in sight,
The ladie counseld him the place to shonne,
Whereas so many knights had fouly bene fordonne.

XXXI

Her fearefull speaches nought he did regard,
But ryding streight under the castle wall,
Called aloud unto the watchfull ward,
Which there did wayte, willing them forth to call
Into the field their tyrants seneschall.
To whom when tydings thereof came, he streight
Cals for his armes, and arming him withall,
Eftsoones forth pricked proudly in his might,
And gan with courage fierce addresse him to the fight.

XXXII

They both encounter in the middle plaine,
And their sharpe speares doe both together smite
Amid their shields, with so huge might and maine,
That seem'd their soules they wold have ryven quight
Out of their breasts, with furious despight.
Yet could the seneschals no entrance find
Into the Princes shield, where it empight,
So pure the mettall was, and well refynd,
But shivered all about, and scattered in the wynd.

XXXIII

Not so the Princes, but with restlesse force
Into his shield it readie passage found,
Both through his haberjeon and eke his corse:
Which tombling downe upon the senselesse ground,
Gave leave unto his ghost from thraldome bound,
To wander in the griesly shades of night.
There did the Prince him leave in deadly swound,
And thence unto the castle marched right,
To see if entrance there as yet obtaine he might.

XXXIV

But as he nigher drew, three knights he spyde,
All arm'd to point, issuing forth a pace,
Which towards him with all their powre did ryde,
And meeting him right in the middle race,
Did all their speares attonce on him enchace.

As three great culverings for battrie bent,
And leveld all against one certaine place,
Doe all attonce their thunders rage forth rent,
That makes the wals to stagger with astonishment.

XXXV
So all attonce they on the Prince did thonder;
Who from his saddle swarved nought asyde,
Ne to their force gave way, that was great wonder,
But like a bulwarke firmely did abyde,
Rebutting him which in the midst did ryde,
With so huge rigour, that his mortall speare
Past through his shield, and pierst through either syde,
That downe he fell uppon his mother deare,
And powred forth his wretched life in deadly dreare.

XXXVI
Whom when his other fellowes saw, they fled
As fast as feete could carry them away;
And after them the Prince as swiftly sped,
To be aveng'd of their unknightly play.
There whilest they, entring, th' one did th' other stay,
The hindmost in the gate he overhent,
And as he pressed in, him there did slay:
His carkasse, tumbling on the threshold, sent
His groning soule unto her place of punishment.

XXXVII
The other, which was entred, laboured fast
To sperre the gate; but that same lumpe of clay,
Whose grudging ghost was thereout fled and past,
Right in the middest of the threshold lay,
That it the posterne did from closing stay:
The whiles the Prince hard preased in betweene,
And entraunce wonne. Streight th' other fled away,
And ran into the hall, where he did weene
Him selfe to save: but he there slew him at the skreene.

XXXVIII
Then all the rest which in that castle were,
Seeing that sad ensample them before,
Durst not abide, but fled away for feare,
And them convayd out at a posterne dore.
Long sought the Prince, but when he found no more
T' oppose against his powre, he forth issued
Unto that lady, where he her had lore,
And her gan cheare with what she there had vewed,
And what she had not seene within unto her shewed.

XXXIX
Who with right humble thankes him goodly greeting,

For so great prowesse as he there had proved,
Much greater then was ever in her weeting,
With great admiraunce inwardly was moved,
And honourd him with all that her behoved.
Thenceforth into that castle he her led,
With her two sonnes, right deare of her beloved,
Where all that night them selves they cherished,
And from her balefull minde all care he banished.

CANTO XI

**Prince Arthure overcomes the great
Gerioneo in fight:
Doth slay the monster, and restore
Belge unto her right.**

I

It often fals in course of common life,
That right long time is overborne of wrong,
Through avarice, or powre, or guile, or strife,
That weakens her, and makes her party strong:
But Justice, though her dome she doe prolong,
Yet at the last she will her owne cause right:
As by sad Belge seemes, whose wrongs though long
She suffred, yet at length she did requight,
And sent redresse thereof by this brave Briton knight.

II

Whereof when newes was to that tyrant brought,
How that the Lady Belge now had found
A champion, that had with his champion fought,
And laid his seneschall low on the ground,
And eke him selfe did threaten to confound,
He gan to burne in rage, and friese in feare,
Doubting sad end of principle unsound:
Yet sith he heard but one that did appeare,
He did him selfe encourage, and take better cheare.

III

Nathelesse him selfe he armed all in hast,
And forth he far'd with all his many bad,
Ne stayed step, till that he came at last
Unto the castle which they conquerd had.
There with huge terrour, to be more ydrad,
He sternely marcht before the castle gate,
And with bold vaunts and ydle threatning bad
Deliver him his owne, ere yet too late,

To which they had no right, nor any wrongfull state.

IV
The Prince staid not his aunswere to devize,
But opening streight the sparre, forth to him came,
Full nobly mounted in right warlike wize;
And asked him, if that he were the same,
Who all that wrong unto that wofull dame
So long had done, and from her native land
Exiled her, that all the world spake shame.
He boldly aunswerd him, he there did stand
That would his doings justifie with his owne hand.

V
With that so furiously at him he flew,
As if he would have overrun him streight,
And with his huge great yron axe gan hew
So hideously uppon his armour bright,
As he to peeces would have chopt it quight:
That the bold Prince was forced foote to give
To his first rage, and yeeld to his despight;
The whilest at him so dreadfully he drive,
That seem'd a marble rocke asunder could have rive.

VI
Thereto a great advauntage eke he has
Through his three double hands thrise multiplyde,
Besides the double strength which in them was:
For stil when fit occasion did betyde,
He could his weapon shift from side to syde,
From hand to hand, and with such nimblesse sly
Could wield about, that ere it were espide,
The wicked stroke did wound his enemy,
Behinde, beside, before, as he it list apply.

VII
Which uncouth use when as the Prince perceived,
He gan to watch the wielding of his hand,
Least by such slight he were unwares deceived;
And ever ere he saw the stroke to land,
He would it meete and warily withstand.
One time, when he his weapon faynd to shift,
As he was wont, and chang'd from hand to hand,
He met him with a counterstroke so swift,
That quite smit off his arme, as he it up did lift.

VIII
Therewith, all fraught with fury and disdaine,
He brayd aloud for very fell despight,
And sodainely t' avenge him selfe againe,
Gan into one assemble all the might

Of all his hands, and heaved them on hight,
Thinking to pay him with that one for all:
But the sad steele seizd not, where it was hight,
Uppon the childe, but somewhat short did fall,
And lighting on his horses head, him quite did mall.

IX
Downe streight to ground fell his astonisht steed,
And eke to th' earth his burden with him bare:
But he him selfe full lightly from him freed,
And gan him selfe to fight on foote prepare.
Whereof when as the gyant was aware,
He wox right blyth, as he had got thereby,
And laught so loud, that all his teeth wide bare
One might have seene enraung'd disorderly,
Like to a rancke of piles, that pitched are awry.

X
Eftsoones againe his axe he raught on hie,
Ere he were throughly buckled to his geare,
And can let drive at him so dreadfullie,
That had he chaunced not his shield to reare,
Ere that huge stroke arrived on him neare,
He had him surely cloven quite in twaine.
But th' adamantine shield which he did beare
So well was tempred, that, for all his maine,
It would no passage yeeld unto his purpose vaine.

XI
Yet was the stroke so forcibly applide,
That made him stagger with uncertaine sway,
As if he would have tottered to one side.
Wherewith full wroth, he fiercely gan assay
That curt'sie with like kindnesse to repay;
And smote at him with so importune might,
That two more of his armes did fall away,
Like fruitlesse braunches, which the hatchets slight
Hath pruned from the native tree, and cropped quight.

XII
With that all mad and furious he grew,
Like a fell mastiffe through enraging heat,
And curst, and band, and blasphemies forth threw
Against his gods, and fire to them did threat,
And hell unto him selfe with horrour great.
Thenceforth he car'd no more which way he strooke,
Nor where it light, but gan to chaufe and sweat,
And gnasht his teeth, and his head at him shooke,
And sternely him beheld with grim and ghastly looke.

XIII

Nought fear'd the childe his lookes, ne yet his threats,
But onely wexed now the more aware,
To save him selfe from those his furious heats,
And watch advauntage, how to worke his care;
The which good fortune to him offred faire.
For as he in his rage him overstrooke,
He, ere he could his weapon backe repaire,
His side all bare and naked overtooke,
And with his mortal steel quite throgh the body strooke.

XIV
Through all three bodies he him strooke attonce,
That all the three attonce fell on the plaine:
Else should he thrise have needed for the nonce
Them to have stricken, and thrise to have slaine.
So now all three one sencelesse lumpe remaine,
Enwallow'd in his owne blacke bloudy gore,
And byting th' earth for very deaths disdaine;
Who, with a cloud of night him covering, bore
Downe to the house of dole, his daies there to deplore.

XV
Which when the lady from the castle saw,
Where she with her two sonnes did looking stand,
She towards him in hast her selfe did draw,
To greet him the good fortune of his hand:
And all the people both of towne and land,
Which there stood gazing from the citties wall
Uppon these warriours, greedy t' understand
To whether should the victory befall,
Now when they saw it falne, they eke him greeted all.

XVI
But Belge with her sonnes prostrated low
Before his feete, in all that peoples sight,
Mongst joyes mixing some tears, mongst wele some wo,
Him thus bespake: 'O most redoubted knight,
The which hast me, of all most wretched wight,
That earst was dead, restor'd to life againe,
And these weake impes replanted by thy might;
What guerdon can I give thee for thy paine,
But even that which thou savedst, thine still to remaine?'

XVII
He tooke her up forby the lilly hand,
And her recomforted the best he might,
Saying: 'Deare lady, deedes ought not be scand
By th' authors manhood, nor the doers might,
But by their trueth and by the causes right:
That same is it, which fought for you this day.
What other meed then need me to requight,

But that which yeeldeth vertues meed alway?
That is the vertue selfe, which her reward doth pay.'

XVIII
She humbly thankt him for that wondrous grace,
And further sayd: 'Ah! sir, but mote ye please,
Sith ye thus farre have tendred my poore case,
As from my chiefest foe me to release,
That your victorious arme will not yet cease,
Till ye have rooted all the relickes out
Of that vilde race, and stablished my peace.'
'What is there else,' sayd he, 'left of their rout?
Declare it boldly, dame, and doe not stand in dout.'

XIX
'Then wote you, sir, that in this church hereby,
There stands an idole of great note and name,
The which this gyant reared first on hie,
And of his owne vaine fancies thought did frame:
To whom, for endlesse horrour of his shame,
He offred up for daily sacrifize
My children and my people, burnt in flame,
With all the tortures that he could devize,
The more t' aggrate his god with such his blouddy guize.

XX
'And underneath this idoll there doth lie
An hideous monster, that doth it defend,
And feedes on all the carkasses that die
In sacrifize unto that cursed feend:
Whose ugly shape none ever saw, nor kend,
That ever scap'd: for of a man they say
It has the voice, that speaches forth doth send,
Even blasphemous words, which she doth bray
Out of her poysnous entrails, fraught with dire decay.'

XXI
Which when the Prince heard tell, his heart gan earne
For great desire, that monster to assay,
And prayd the place of her abode to learne.
Which being shew'd, he gan him selfe streight way
Thereto addresse, and his bright shield display.
So to the church he came, where it was told
The monster underneath the altar lay;
There he that idoll saw of massy gold
Most richly made, but there no monster did behold.

XXII
Upon the image with his naked blade
Three times, as in defiance, there he strooke;
And the third time, out of an hidden shade,

There forth issewd, from under th' altars smooke,
A dreadfull feend, with fowle deformed looke,
That stretcht it selfe, as it had long lyen still;
And her long taile and fethers strongly shooke,
That all the temple did with terrour fill;
Yet him nought terrifide, that feared nothing ill.

XXIII
An huge great beast it was, when it in length
Was stretched forth, that nigh fild all the place,
And seem'd to be of infinite great strength;
Horrible, hideous, and of hellish race,
Borne of the brooding of Echidna base,
Or other like infernall Furies kinde:
For of a mayd she had the outward face,
To hide the horrour which did lurke behinde,
The better to beguile whom she so fond did finde.

XXIV
Thereto the body of a dog she had,
Full of fell ravin and fierce greedinesse;
A lions clawes, with powre and rigour clad,
To rend and teare what so she can oppresse;
A dragons taile, whose sting without redresse
Full deadly wounds, where so it is empight;
And eagles wings, for scope and speedinesse,
That nothing may escape her reaching might,
Whereto she ever list to make her hardy flight.

XXV
Much like in foulnesse and deformity
Unto that monster whom the Theban knight,
The father of that fatall progeny,
Made kill her selfe for very hearts despight,
That he had red her riddle, which no wight
Could ever loose, but suffred deadly doole.
So also did this monster use like slight
To many a one which came unto her schoole,
Whom she did put to death, deceved like a foole.

XXVI
She comming forth, when as she first beheld
The armed Prince, with shield so blazing bright,
Her ready to assaile, was greatly queld,
And much dismayd with that dismayfull sight,
That backe she would have turnd for great affright.
But he gan her with courage fierce assay,
That forst her turne againe in her despight,
To save her selfe, least that he did her slay:
And sure he had her slaine, had she not turnd her way.

XXVII
Tho, when she saw that she was forst to fight,
She flew at him, like to an hellish feend,
And on his shield tooke hold with all her might,
As if that it she would in peeces rend,
Or reave out of the hand that did it hend.
Strongly he strove out of her greedy gripe
To loose his shield, and long while did contend:
But when he could not quite it, with one stripe
Her lions clawes he from her feete away did wipe.

XXVIII
With that aloude she gan to bray and yell,
And fowle blasphemous speaches forth did cast,
And bitter curses, horrible to tell,
That even the temple, wherein she was plast,
Did quake to heare, and nigh asunder brast.
Tho with her huge long taile she at him strooke,
That made him stagger, and stand halfe agast
With trembling joynts, as he for terrour shooke;
Who nought was terrifide, but greater courage tooke.

XXIX
As when the mast of some well timbred hulke
Is with the blast of some outragious storme
Blowne downe, it shakes the bottome of the bulke,
And makes her ribs to cracke, as they were torne,
Whilest still she stands as stonisht and forlorne:
So was he stound with stroke of her huge taile.
But ere that it she backe againe had borne,
He with his sword it strooke, that without faile
He joynted it, and mard the swinging of her flaile.

XXX
Then gan she cry much louder then afore,
That all the people there without it heard,
And Belge selfe was therewith stonied sore,
As if the onely sound thereof she feard.
But then the feend her selfe more fiercely reard
Uppon her wide great wings, and strongly flew
With all her body at his head and beard,
That had he not foreseene with heedfull vew,
And thrown his shield atween, she had him done to rew.

XXXI
But as she prest on him with heavy sway,
Under her wombe his fatall sword he thrust,
And for her entrailes made an open way
To issue forth; the which, once being brust,
Like to a great mill damb forth fiercely gusht,
And powred out of her infernall sinke

Most ugly filth, and poyson therewith rusht,
That him nigh choked with the deadly stinke:
Such loathly matter were small lust to speake, or thinke.

XXXII
Then downe to ground fell that deformed masse,
Breathing out clouds of sulphure fowle and blacke,
In which a puddle of contagion was,
More loathd then Lerna, or then Stygian lake,
That any man would nigh awhaped make.
Whom when he saw on ground, he was full glad,
And streight went forth his gladnesse to partake
With Belge, who watcht all this while full sad,
Wayting what end would be of that same daunger drad.

XXXIII
Whom when she saw so joyously come forth,
She gan rejoyce, and shew triumphant chere,
Lauding and praysing his renowmed worth
By all the names that honorable were.
Then in he brought her, and her shewed there
The present of his paines, that monsters spoyle,
And eke that idoll deem'd so costly dere;
Whom he did all to peeces breake, and foyle
In filthy durt, and left so in the loathely soyle.

XXXIV
Then all the people, which beheld that day,
Gan shout aloud, that unto heaven it rong;
And all the damzels of that towne in ray
Came dauncing forth, and joyous carrols song:
So him they led through all their streetes along,
Crowned with girlonds of immortall baies,
And all the vulgar did about them throng,
To see the man, whose everlasting praise
They all were bound to all posterities to raise.

XXXV
There he with Belgæ did a while remaine,
Making great feast and joyous merriment,
Untill he had her settled in her raine,
With safe assuraunce and establishment.
Then to his first emprize his mind he lent,
Full loath to Belgæ and to all the rest:
Of whom yet taking leave, thenceforth he went
And to his former journey him addrest,
On which long way he rode, ne ever day did rest.

XXXVI
But turne we now to noble Artegall;
Who, having left Mercilla, streight way went

On his first quest, the which him forth did call,
To weet, to worke Irenaes franchisement,
And eke Grantortoes worthy punishment.
So forth he fared as his manner was,
With onely Talus wayting diligent,
Through many perils and much way did pas,
Till nigh unto the place at length approcht he has.

XXXVII
There as he traveld by the way, he met
An aged wight, wayfaring all alone,
Who through his yeares long since aside had set
The use of armes, and battell quite forgone:
To whom as he approcht, he knew anone
That it was he which whilome did attend
On faire Irene in her affliction,
When first to Faery court he saw her wend,
Unto his Soveraine Queene her suite for to commend.

XXXVIII
Whom by his name saluting, thus he gan:
'Haile, good Sir Sergis, truest knight alive,
Well tride in all thy ladies troubles than
When her that tyrant did of crowne deprive;
What new ocasion doth thee hither drive,
Whiles she alone is left, and thou here found?
Or is she thrall, or doth she not survive?'
To whom he thus: 'She liveth sure and sound;
But by that tyrant is in wretched thraldome bound.

XXXIX
'For she, presuming on th' appointed tyde,
In which ye promist, as ye were a knight,
To meete her at the Salvage Ilands syde,
And then and there for triall of her right
With her unrighteous enemy to fight,
Did thither come, where she, afrayd of nought,
By guilefull treason and by subtill slight
Surprized was, and to Grantorto brought,
Who her imprisond hath, and her life often sought.

XL
'And now he hath to her prefixt a day,
By which if that no champion doe appeare,
Which will her cause in battailous array
Against him justifie, and prove her cleare
Of all those crimes that he gainst her doth reare,
She death shall sure aby.' Those tidings sad
Did much abash Sir Artegall to heare,
And grieved sore, that through his fault she had
Fallen into that tyrants hand and usage bad.

XLI
Then thus replide: 'Now sure and by my life,
Too much am I too blame for that faire maide,
That have her drawne to all this troublous strife,
Through promise to afford her timely aide,
Which by default I have not yet defraide.
But witnesse unto me, ye heavens, that know
How cleare I am from blame of this upbraide:
For ye into like thraldome me did throw,
And kept from complishing the faith which I did owe.

XLII
'But now aread, Sir Sergis, how long space
Hath he her lent, a champion to provide.'
'Ten daies,' quoth he, 'he graunted hath of grace,
For that he weeneth well, before that tide
None can have tidings to assist her side.
For all the shores, which to the sea accoste,
He day and night doth ward both far and wide,
That none can there arrive without an hoste:
So her he deemes already but a damned ghoste.'

XLIII
'Now turne againe,' Sir Artegall then sayd;
'For if I live till those ten daies have end,
Assure your selfe, sir knight, she shall have ayd,
Though I this dearest life for her doe spend.'
So backeward he attone with him did wend.
Tho, as they rode together on their way,
A rout of people they before them kend,
Flocking together in confusde array,
As if that there were some tumultuous affray.

XLIV
To which as they approcht, the cause to know,
They saw a knight in daungerous distresse
Of a rude rout him chasing to and fro,
That sought with lawlesse powre him to oppresse,
And bring in bondage of their brutishnesse:
And farre away, amid their rakehell bands,
They spide a lady left all succourlesse,
Crying, and holding up her wretched hands
To him for aide, who long in vaine their rage withstands.

XLV
Yet still he strives, ne any perill spares,
To reskue her from their rude violence,
And like a lion wood amongst them fares,
Dealing his dreadfull blowes with large dispence,
Gainst which the pallid death findes no defence.

But all in vaine; their numbers are so great,
That naught may boot to banishe them from thence:
For soone as he their outrage backe doth beat,
They turne afresh, and oft renew their former threat.

XLVI
And now they doe so sharpely him assay,
That they his shield in peeces battred have,
And forced him to throw it quite away,
Fro dangers dread his doubtfull life to save;
Albe that it most safety to him gave,
And much did magnifie his noble name:
For from the day that he thus did it leave,
Amongst all knights he blotted was with blame,
And counted but a recreant knight, with endles shame.

XLVII
Whom when they thus distressed did behold,
They drew unto his aide; but that rude rout
Them also gan assaile with outrage bold,
And forced them, how ever strong and stout
They were, as well approv'd in many a doubt,
Backe to recule; untill that yron man
With his huge flaile began to lay about,
From whose sterne presence they diffused ran,
Like scattred chaffe, the which the wind away doth fan.

XLVIII
So when that knight from perill cleare was freed,
He, drawing neare, began to greete them faire,
And yeeld great thankes for their so goodly deed,
In saving him from daungerous despaire
Of those which sought his life for to empaire.
Of whom Sir Artegall gan then enquire
The whole occasion of his late misfare,
And who he was, and what those villaines were,
The which with mortall malice him pursu'd so nere.

XLIX
To whom he thus: 'My name is Burbon hight,
Well knowne, and far renowmed heretofore,
Untill late mischiefe did uppon me light,
That all my former praise hath blemisht sore;
And that faire lady, which in that uprore
Ye with those caytives saw, Flourdelis hight,
Is mine owne love, though me she have forlore,
Whether withheld from me by wrongfull might,
Or with her owne good will, I cannot read aright.

L
'But sure to me her faith she first did plight,

To be my love, and take me for her lord,
Till that a tyrant, which Grandtorto hight,
With golden giftes and many a guilefull word
Entyced her, to him for to accord.
O who may not with gifts and words be tempted?
Sith which she hath me ever since abhord,
And to my foe hath guilefully consented:
Ay me, that ever guyle in wemen was invented!

LI
'And now he hath this troupe of villains sent,
By open force to fetch her quite away:
Gainst whom my selfe I long in vaine have bent
To rescue her, and daily meanes assay,
Yet rescue her thence by no meanes I may:
For they doe me with multitude oppresse,
And with unequall might doe overlay,
That oft I driven am to great distresse,
And forced to forgoe th' attempt remedilesse.'

LII
'But why have ye,' said Artegall, 'forborne
Your owne good shield in daungerous dismay?
That is the greatest shame and foulest scorne,
Which unto any knight behappen may,
To loose the badge that should his deedes display.'
To whom Sir Burbon, blushing halfe for shame,
'That shall I unto you,' quoth he, 'bewray;
Least ye therefore mote happily me blame,
And deeme it doen of will, that through inforcement came.

LIII
'True is, that I at first was dubbed knight
By a good knight, the Knight of the Redcrosse;
Who when he gave me armes, in field to fight,
Gave me a shield, in which he did endosse
His deare Redeemers badge upon the bosse:
The same long while I bore, and therewithall
Fought many battels without wound or losse;
Therewith Grandtorto selfe I did appall,
And made him oftentimes in field before me fall.

LIV
'But for that many did that shield envie,
And cruell enemies increased more;
To stint all strife and troublous enmitie,
That bloudie scutchin being battered sore,
I layd aside, and have of late forbore,
Hoping thereby to have my love obtayned:
Yet can I not my love have nathemore;
For she by force is still fro me detayned,

And with corruptfull brybes is to untruth mis-trayned.'

LV
To whom thus Artegall: 'Certes, sir knight,
Hard is the case the which ye doe complaine;
Yet not so hard (for nought so hard may light,
That it to such a streight mote you constraine)
As to abandon that which doth containe
Your honours stile, that is your warlike shield.
All perill ought be lesse, and lesse all paine,
Then losse of fame in disaventrous field:
Dye rather, then doe ought that mote dishonour yield.'

LVI
'Not so,' quoth he; 'for yet, when time doth serve,
My former shield I may resume againe:
To temporize is not from truth to swerve,
Ne for advantage terme to entertaine,
When as necessitie doth it constraine.'
'Fie on such forgerie,' said Artegall,
'Under one hood to shadow faces twaine!
Knights ought be true, and truth is one in all:
Of all things, to dissemble fouly may befall.'

LVII
'Yet let me you of courtesie request,'
Said Burbon, 'to assist me now at need
Against these pesants which have me opprest,
And forced me to so infamous deed,
That yet my love may from their hands be freed.'
Sir Artegall, albe he earst did wyte
His wavering mind, yet to his aide agreed,
And buckling him eftsoones unto the fight,
Did set upon those troupes with all his powre and might.

LVIII
Who flocking round about them, as a swarme
Of flyes upon a birchen bough doth cluster,
Did them assault with terrible allarme,
And over all the fields themselves did muster,
With bils and glayves making a dreadfull luster;
That forst at first those knights backe to retyre:
As when the wrathfull Boreas doth bluster,
Nought may abide the tempest of his yre;
Both man and beast doe fly, and succour doe inquyre.

LIX
But when as overblowen was that brunt,
Those knights began a fresh them to assayle,
And all about the fields like squirrels hunt;
But chiefly Talus with his yron flayle,

Gainst which no flight nor rescue mote avayle,
Made cruell havocke of the baser crew,
And chaced them both over hill and dale:
The raskall manie soone they overthrew,
But the two knights themselves their captains did subdew.

LX
At last they came whereas that ladie bode,
Whom now her keepers had forsaken quight,
To save themselves, and scattered were abrode:
Her halfe dismayd they found in doubtfull plight,
As neither glad nor sorie for their sight;
Yet wondrous faire she was, and richly clad
In roiall robes, and many jewels dight,
But that those villens through their usage bad
Them fouly rent and shamefully defaced had.

LXI
But Burbon, streight dismounting from his steed,
Unto her ran with greedie great desyre,
And catching her fast by her ragged weed,
Would have embraced her with hart entyre.
But she, backstarting with disdainefull yre,
Bad him avaunt, ne would unto his lore
Allured be, for prayer nor for meed.
Whom when those knights so froward and forlore
Beheld, they her rebuked and upbrayded sore.

LXII
Sayd Artegall: 'What foule disgrace is this
To so faire ladie as ye seeme in sight,
To blot your beautie, that unblemisht is,
With so foule blame as breach of faith once plight,
Or change of love for any worlds delight!
Is ought on earth so pretious or deare,
As prayse and honour? Or is ought so bright
And beautifull as glories beames appeare,
Whose goodly light then Phebus lampe doth shine more cleare?

LXIII
'Why then will ye, fond dame, attempted bee
Unto a strangers love, so lightly placed,
For guiftes of gold or any worldly glee,
To leave the love that ye before embraced,
And let your fame with falshood be defaced?
Fie on the pelfe for which good name is sold,
And honour with indignitie debased!
Dearer is love then life, and fame then gold;
But dearer then them both your faith once plighted hold.'

LXIV

Much was the ladie in her gentle mind
Abasht at his rebuke, that bit her neare,
Ne ought to answere thereunto did find;
But hanging downe her head with heavie cheare,
Stood long amaz'd, as she amated weare.
Which Burbon seeing, her againe assayd,
And clasping twixt his armes, her up did reare
Upon his steede, whiles she no whit gainesayd;
So bore her quite away, nor well nor ill apayd.

LXV
Nathlesse the yron man did still pursew
That raskall many with unpittied spoyle,
Ne ceassed not, till all their scattred crew
Into the sea he drove quite from that soyle,
The which they troubled had with great turmoyle.
But Artegall, seeing his cruell deed,
Commaunded him from slaughter to recoyle,
And to his voyage gan againe proceed:
For that the terme, approching fast, required speed.

CANTO XII

Artegall doth Sir Burbon aide,
And blames for changing shield:
He with the great Grantorto fights,
And slaieth him in field.

I
O sacred hunger of ambitious mindes,
And impotent desire of men to raine,
Whom neither dread of God, that devils bindes,
Nor lawes of men, that common weales containe,
Nor bands of nature, that wilde beastes restraine,
Can keepe from outrage and from doing wrong,
Where they may hope a kingdome to obtaine.
No faith so firme, no trust can be so strong,
No love so lasting then, that may enduren long.

II
Witnesse may Burbon be, whom all the bands
Which may a knight assure had surely bound,
Untill the love of lordship and of lands
Made him become most faithlesse and unsound:
And witnesse be Gerioneo found,
Who for like cause faire Belge did oppresse,
And right and wrong most cruelly confound:

And so be now Grantorto, who no lesse
Then all the rest burst out to all outragiousnesse.

III
Gainst whom Sir Artegall, long having since
Taken in hand th' exploit, being theretoo
Appointed by that mightie Faerie prince,
Great Gloriane, that tyrant to fordoo,
Through other great adventures hethertoo
Had it forslackt. But now time drawing ny,
To him assynd, her high beheast to doo,
To the sea shore he gan his way apply,
To weete if shipping readie he mote there descry.

IV
Tho, when they came to the sea coast, they found
A ship all readie (as good fortune fell)
To put to sea, with whom they did compound
To passe them over, where them list to tell:
The winde and weather served them so well,
That in one day they with the coast did fall;
Whereas they readie found, them to repell,
Great hostes of men in order martiall,
Which them forbad to land, and footing did forstall.

V
But nathemore would they from land refraine,
But when as nigh unto the shore they drew,
That foot of man might sound the bottome plaine,
Talus into the sea did forth issew,
Though darts from shore and stones they at him threw;
And wading through the waves with stedfast sway,
Maugre the might of all those troupes in vew,
Did win the shore, whence he them chast away,
And made to fly, like doves whom the eagle doth affray.

VI
The whyles Sir Artegall with that old knight
Did forth descend, there being none them neare,
And forward marched to a towne in sight.
By this came tydings to the tyrants eare,
By those which earst did fly away for feare,
Of their arrivall: wherewith troubled sore,
He all his forces streight to him did reare,
And forth issuing with his scouts afore,
Meant them to have incountred, ere they left the shore.

VII
But ere he marched farre, he with them met,
And fiercely charged them with all his force;
But Talus sternely did upon them set,

And brusht and battred them without remorse,
That on the ground he left full many a corse;
Ne any able was him to withstand,
But he them overthrew both man and horse,
That they lay scattred over all the land,
As thicke as doth the seede after the sowers hand.

VIII
Till Artegall, him seeing so to rage,
Willd him to stay, and signe of truce did make:
To which all harkning, did a while asswage
Their forces furie, and their terror slake;
Till he an herauld cald, and to him spake,
Willing him wend unto the tyrant streight,
And tell him that not for such slaughters sake
He thether came, but for to trie the right
Of fayre Irenaes cause with him in single fight:

IX
And willed him for to reclayme with speed
His scattred people, ere they all were slaine,
And time and place convenient to agreed,
In which they two the combat might darraine.
Which message when Grantorto heard, full fayne
And glad he was the slaughter so to stay,
And pointed for the combat twixt them twayne
The morrow next, ne gave him longer day:
So sounded the retraite, and drew his folke away.

X
That night Sir Artegall did cause his tent
There to be pitched on the open plaine;
For he had given streight commaundement,
That none should dare him once to entertaine:
Which none durst breake, though many would right faine
For fayre Irena, whom they loved deare.
But yet old Sergis did so well him paine,
That from close friends, that dar'd not to appeare,
He all things did purvay, which for them needfull weare.

XI
The morrow next, that was the dismall day
Appointed for Irenas death before,
So soone as it did to the world display
His chearefull face, and light to men restore,
The heavy mayd, to whom none tydings bore
Of Artegals arryvall, her to free,
Lookt up with eyes full sad and hart full sore;
Weening her lifes last howre then neare to bee,
Sith no redemption nigh she did nor heare nor see.

XII
Then up she rose, and on her selfe did dight
Most squalid garments, fit for such a day,
And with dull countenance, and with doleful spright,
She forth was brought in sorrowfull dismay,
For to receive the doome of her decay.
But comming to the place, and finding there
Sir Artegall, in battailous array
Wayting his foe, it did her dead hart cheare,
And new life to her lent, in midst of deadly feare.

XIII
Like as a tender rose in open plaine,
That with untimely drought nigh withered was,
And hung the head, soone as few drops of raine
Thereon distill, and deaw her daintie face,
Gins to looke up, and with fresh wonted grace
Dispreds the glorie of her leaves gay;
Such was Irenas countenance, such her case,
When Artegall she saw in that array,
There wayting for the tyrant, till it was farre day.

XIV
Who came at length, with proud presumpteous gate,
Into the field, as if he fearelesse were,
All armed in a cote of yron plate,
Of great defence to ward the deadly feare,
And on his head a steele cap he did weare
Of colour rustie browne, but sure and strong;
And in his hand an huge polaxe did beare,
Whose steale was yron studded, but not long,
With which he wont to fight, to justifie his wrong.

XV
Of stature huge and hideous he was,
Like to a giant for his monstrous hight,
And did in strength most sorts of men surpas,
Ne ever any found his match in might;
Thereto he had great skill in single fight:
His face was ugly and his countenance sterne,
That could have frayd one with the very sight,
And gaped like a gulfe when he did gerne,
That whether man or monster one could scarse discerne.

XVI
Soone as he did within the listes appeare,
With dreadfull looke he Artegall beheld,
As if he would have daunted him with feare,
And grinning griesly, did against him weld
His deadly weapon, which in hand he held.
But th' Elfin swayne, that oft had seene like sight,

Was with his ghastly count'nance nothing queld,
But gan him streight to buckle to the fight,
And cast his shield about, to be in readie plight.

XVII
The trompets sound, and they together goe,
With dreadfull terror and with fell intent;
And their huge strokes full daungerously bestow,
To doe most dammage where as most they ment.
But with such force and furie violent
The tyrant thundred his thicke blowes so fast,
That through the yron walles their way they rent,
And even to the vitall parts they past,
Ne ought could them endure, but all they cleft or brast.

XVIII
Which cruell outrage when as Artegall
Did well avize, thenceforth with warie heed
He shund his strokes, where ever they did fall,
And way did give unto their gracelesse speed:
As when a skilfull marriner doth reed
A storme approching, that doth perill threat,
He will not bide the daunger of such dread,
But strikes his sayles, and vereth his mainsheat,
And lends unto it leave the emptie ayre to beat.

XIX
So did the Faerie knight himselfe abeare,
And stouped oft, his head from shame to shield;
No shame to stoupe, ones head more high to reare,
And, much to gaine, a litle for to yield;
So stoutest knights doen oftentimes in field.
But still the tyrant sternely at him layd,
And did his yron axe so nimbly wield,
That many wounds into his flesh it made,
And with his burdenous blowes him sore did overlade.

XX
Yet when as fit advantage he did spy,
The whiles the cursed felon high did reare
His cruell hand, to smite him mortally,
Under his stroke he to him stepping neare,
Right in the flanke him strooke with deadly dreare,
That the gore bloud, thence gushing grievously,
Did underneath him like a pond appeare,
And all his armour did with purple dye:
Thereat he brayed loud, and yelled dreadfully.

XXI
Yet the huge stroke, which he before intended,
Kept on his course, as he did it direct,

And with such monstrous poise adowne descended,
That seemed nought could him from death protect:
But he it well did ward with wise respect,
And twixt him and the blow his shield did cast,
Which thereon seizing, tooke no great effect,
But byting deepe therein did sticke so fast,
That by no meanes it backe againe he forth could wrast.

XXII
Long while he tug'd and strove, to get it out,
And all his powre applyed thereunto,
That he therewith the knight drew all about:
Nathlesse, for all that ever he could doe,
His axe he could not from his shield undoe.
Which Artegall perceiving, strooke no more,
But loosing soone his shield, did it forgoe,
And whiles he combred was therewith so sore,
He gan at him let drive more fiercely then afore.

XXIII
So well he him pursew'd, that at the last
He stroke him with Chrysaor on the hed,
That with the souse thereof full sore aghast,
He staggered to and fro in doubtfull sted.
Againe, whiles he him saw so ill bested,
He did him smite with all his might and maine,
That, falling, on his mother earth he fed:
Whom when he saw prostrated on the plaine,
He lightly reft his head, to ease him of his paine.

XXIV
Which when the people round about him saw,
They shouted all for joy of his successe,
Glad to be quit from that proud tyrants awe,
Which with strong powre did them long time oppresse;
And running all with greedie joyfulnesse
To faire Irena, at her feet did fall,
And her adored with due humblenesse,
As their true liege and princesse naturall;
And eke her champions glorie sounded over all.

XXV
Who streight her leading with meete majestie
Unto the pallace, where their kings did rayne,
Did her therein establish peaceablie,
And to her kingdomes seat restore agayne.
And all such persons as did late maintayne
That tyrants part, with close or open ayde,
He sorely punished with heavie payne;
That in short space, whiles there with her he stayd,
Not one was left that durst her once have disobayd.

XXVI
During which time that he did there remaine,
His studie was true justice how to deale,
And day and night employ'd his busie paine
How to reforme that ragged common-weale:
And that same yron man, which could reveale
All hidden crimes, through all that realme he sent,
To search out those that usd to rob and steale,
Or did rebell gainst lawfull government;
On whom he did inflict most grievous punishment.

XXVII
But ere he could reforme it thoroughly,
He through occasion called was away
To Faerie court, that of necessity
His course of justice he was forst to stay,
And Talus to revoke from the right way,
In which he was that realme for to redresse.
But envies cloud still dimmeth vertues ray.
So having freed Irena from distresse,
He tooke his leave of her, there left in heavinesse.

XXVIII
Tho, as he backe returned from that land,
And there arriv'd againe, whence forth he set,
He had not passed farre upon the strand,
When as two old ill favour'd hags he met,
By the way side being together set;
Two griesly creatures; and, to that their faces
Most foule and filthie were, their garments yet,
Being all rag'd and tatter'd, their disgraces
Did much the more augment, and made most ugly cases.

XXIX
The one of them, that elder did appeare,
With her dull eyes did seeme to looke askew,
That her mis-shape much helpt; and her foule heare
Hung loose and loathsomely: thereto her hew
Was wan and leane, that all her teeth arew
And all her bones might through her cheekes be red;
Her lips were like raw lether, pale and blew,
And as she spake, therewith she slavered;
Yet spake she seldom, but thought more, the lesse she sed.

XXX
Her hands were foule and durtie, never washt
In all her life, with long nayles over raught,
Like puttocks clawes: with th' one of which she scracht
Her cursed head, although it itched naught;
The other held a snake with venime fraught,

On which she fed and gnawed hungrily,
As if that long she had not eaten ought;
That round about her jawes one might descry
The bloudie gore and poyson dropping lothsomely.

XXXI
Her name was Envie, knowen well thereby;
Whose nature is to grieve and grudge at all
That ever she sees doen prays-worthily,
Whose sight to her is greatest crosse may fall,
And vexeth so, that makes her eat her gall.
For when she wanteth other thing to eat,
She feedes on her owne maw unnaturall,
And of her owne foule entrayles makes her meat;
Meat fit for such a monsters monsterous dyeat.

XXXII
And if she hapt of any good to heare,
That had to any happily betid,
Then would she inly fret, and grieve, and teare
Her flesh for felnesse, which she inward hid:
But if she heard of ill that any did,
Or harme that any had, then would she make
Great cheare, like one unto a banquet bid;
And in anothers losse great pleasure take,
As she had got thereby, and gayned a great stake.

XXXIII
The other nothing better was then shee;
Agreeing in bad will and cancred kynd,
But in bad maner they did disagree:
For what so Envie good or bad did fynd
She did conceale, and murder her owne mynd;
But this, what ever evill she conceived,
Did spred abroad, and throw in th' open wynd.
Yet this in all her words might be perceived,
That all she sought was mens good name to have bereaved.

XXXIV
For what soever good by any sayd
Or doen she heard, she would streightwayes invent
How to deprave, or slaunderously upbrayd,
Or to misconstrue of a mans intent,
And turne to ill the thing that well was ment.
Therefore she used often to resort
To common haunts, and companies frequent,
To hearke what any one did good report,
To blot the same with blame, or wrest in wicked sort.

XXXV
And if that any ill she heard of any,

She would it eeke, and make much worse by telling,
And take great joy to publish it to many,
That every matter worse was for her melling.
Her name was hight Detraction, and her dwelling
Was neare to Envie, even her neighbour next;
A wicked hag, and Envy selfe excelling
In mischiefe: for her selfe she onely vext;
But this same both her selfe and others eke perplext.

XXXVI
Her face was ugly, and her mouth distort,
Foming with poyson round about her gils,
In which her cursed tongue full sharpe and short
Appear'd like aspis sting, that closely kils,
Or cruelly does wound, whom so she wils:
A distaffe in her other hand she had,
Upon the which she litle spinnes, but spils,
And faynes to weave false tales and leasings bad,
To throw amongst the good, which others had disprad.

XXXVII
These two now had themselves combynd in one,
And linckt together gainst Sir Artegall,
For whom they wayted as his mortall fone,
How they might make him into mischiefe fall,
For freeing from their snares Irena thrall:
Besides, unto themselves they gotten had
A monster, which the Blatant Beast men call,
A dreadfull feend, of gods and men ydrad,
Whom they by slights allur'd, and to their purpose lad.

XXXVIII
Such were these hags, and so unhandsome drest:
Who when they nigh approching had espyde
Sir Artegall, return'd from his late quest,
They both arose, and at him loudly cryde,
As it had bene two shepheards curres had scryde
A ravenous wolfe amongst the scattered flocks.
And Envie first, as she that first him eyde,
Towardes him runs, and with rude flaring lockes
About her eares, does beat her brest and forhead knockes.

XXXIX
Then from her mouth the gobbet she does take,
The which whyleare she was so greedily
Devouring, even that halfe-gnawen snake,
And at him throwes it most despightfully.
The cursed serpent, though she hungrily
Earst chawd thereon, yet was not all so dead,
But that some life remaynd secretly,
And as he past afore withouten dread,

Bit him behind, that long the marke was to be read.

XL
Then th' other comming neare, gan him revile
And fouly rayle, with all she could invent;
Saying that he had with unmanly guile
And foule abusion both his honour blent,
And that bright sword, the sword of Justice lent,
Had stayned with reprochfull crueltie
In guiltlesse blood of many an innocent:
As for Grandtorto, him with treacherie
And traynes having surpriz'd, he fouly did to die.

XLI
Thereto the Blatant Beast, by them set on,
At him began aloud to barke and bay,
With bitter rage and fell contention,
That all the woods and rockes nigh to that way
Began to quake and tremble with dismay,
And all the aire rebellowed againe,
So dreadfully his hundred tongues did bray:
And evermore those hags them selves did paine
To sharpen him, and their owne cursed tongs did straine.

XLII
And still among, most bitter wordes they spake,
Most shamefull, most unrighteous, most untrew,
That they the mildest man alive would make
Forget his patience, and yeeld vengeaunce dew
To her, that so false sclaunders at him threw.
And more to make them pierce and wound more deepe,
She with the sting which in her vile tongue grew
Did sharpen them, and in fresh poyson steepe:
Yet he past on, and seem'd of them to take no keepe.

XLIII
But Talus, hearing her so lewdly raile,
And speake so ill of him that well deserved,
Would her have chastiz'd with his yron flaile,
If her Sir Artegall had not preserved,
And him forbidden, who his heast observed.
So much the more at him still did she scold,
And stones did cast; yet he for nought would swerve
From his right course, but still the way did hold
To Faery court, where what him fell shall else be told.

Edmund Spenser – A Short Biography

One of the greatest of English poets, Edmund Spenser was born in East Smithfield, London, in 1552, though an exact date is not recorded.

As a boy, he was educated in London at the Merchant Taylors' School and later at Pembroke College, Cambridge.

As a young man, in 1578, the young Edmund was, for a short time, secretary to John Young, the Bishop of Rochester.

In 1579, he published The Shepheardes Calender, his first major work. The poem follows Colin Clout, a folk character originated by John Skelton, and depicts his life as a shepherd through the twelve months of the year.

It is also around this time that Edmund was married for the first time to Machabyas Childe. The union produced two children; Sylvanus and Katherine.

Edmund journeyed to Ireland in July 1580, in the service of the newly appointed Lord Deputy, Arthur Grey, 14th Baron Grey de Wilton. His time included the terrible massacre at the Siege of Smerwick, though this event seems to have settled his views somewhat on Ireland and the Irish. (The Siege of Smerwick took place at Ard na Caithne in 1580, during the Second Desmond Rebellion. A 400–500 strong force of Papal soldiers captured the town but were later forced to retreat to nearby Dún an Óir, where they were besieged by the English Army and eventually surrendered. On the orders of the English Commander most were then massacred).

When Lord Grey was recalled to England, Edmund stayed, having being appointed to several other official posts and lands in the Munster Plantation. Between 1587 and 1589, Spenser acquired his main estate at Kilcolman, near Doneraile in North Cork.

He later bought a second holding to the south, at Rennie, on a rock overlooking the river Blackwater but still in North Cork. Its ruins are still visible today. A short distance away grew a tree, locally known as "Spenser's Oak". Local legend has it that he penned some of The Faerie Queene under this very tree.

This epic poem, The Faerie Queene, is acknowledged as Edmund's masterpiece. The first three books were published in 1590, and a second set of three books were published in 1596. The original idea was for the poem to consist of twelve books. So although the version we publish here is all that he actually wrote it is still one of the longest, and most magnificent, poems in English literature.

The Faerie Queene is a work on several levels of allegory, including as praise of Queen Elizabeth I. The poem follows several knights in an examination of several virtues. In Spenser's "A Letter of the Authors," he states that the entire epic poem is "cloudily enwrapped in allegorical devises," and that the aim behind The Faerie Queene was to "fashion a gentleman or noble person in virtuous and gentle discipline."

On its publication Spenser travelled to London to publish and promote the work. In this endeavour he was successful enough to obtain a life pension of £50 a year from the Queen who did not give these out lightly.

Spenser used a verse form, now called the Spenserian stanza, in The Faerie Queene as well as several others poems. The stanza's main meter is iambic pentameter with a final line in iambic hexameter (having six stresses, known as an Alexandrine). He was also to use his own rhyme scheme for the sonnet. In a Spenserian sonnet, the last line of every stanza is linked with the first line of the next one.

Spenser was well read in classical literature and strove to emulate such Roman poets as Virgil and Ovid, whom he had studied during his schooling.

Indeed the reality is that Spenser, through his great talents, was able to move Poetry in a different direction. It led to him being called a Poet's Poet and brought rich admiration from Milton, Raleigh, Blake, Wordsworth, Keats, Byron, and Lord Tennyson, among others. John Milton in his Areopagitica called Spenser "our sage and serious poet . . . whom I dare be known to think a better teacher than Scotus or Aquinas".

He had hoped this praise and pension might lead to a position at Court but his next work antagonised the queen's principal secretary, Lord Burghley, through the inclusion of the satirical Mother Hubberd's Tale.

Spenser returned to Ireland and in 1591, Complaints, a collection of poems that voices complaints in mournful or mocking tones was published.

By 1594, Spenser's first wife, Machabyas, had died. Very soon he married Elizabeth Boyle, and to which he dedicated the sonnet sequence Amoretti. The marriage itself was celebrated in Epithalamion and the fruit of this relationship was a son, Peregrine.

In 1595, Spenser now published Amoretti and Epithalamion. The volume contains eighty-nine sonnets.

In the following year Spenser released Prothalamion, a wedding song written for the daughters of a duke, allegedly in hopes to gain favour in the court. More importantly he also wrote a prose pamphlet titled A View of the Present State of Ireland (A Veue of the Present State of Irelande). It was circulated in manuscript form due to its highly inflammatory content. Its main argument was that Ireland would never be totally 'pacified' by the English until its indigenous language and customs had been destroyed, if necessary by violence.

Spenser was a strong proponent of, and wished devoutly, that the Irish language should be eradicated, writing that if children learn Irish before English, "Soe that the speach being Irish, the hart must needes be Irishe; for out of the aboundance of the hart, the tonge speaketh".

He further discussed in the pamphlet future draconian plans to subjugate Ireland, after the most recent rising, led by Hugh O'Neill, having again shown the failure of previous efforts. The work is also a partial defence of Lord Arthur Grey de Wilton, with whom Spenser previously served and who deeply influenced Spenser's views on Ireland.

The goal of this piece was to show that Ireland was in great need of reform. Spenser believed that "Ireland is a diseased portion of the State, it must first be cured and reformed, before it could be in a position to appreciate the good sound laws and blessings of the nation". Spenser categorises the "evils" of the Irish people into three distinct categories: laws, customs, and religion. These three elements work together in creating the disruptive and degraded people. One example given in the work is the native law system called "Brehon Law" which trumps the established law given by the English monarchy. This system has its own court and way of dealing with troubles. It has been passed down through the generations and Spenser views this system as a native and backward custom which must be destroyed. (As an example the Brehon Law methods of dealing with murder by imposing an éraic, or fine, on the murderer's whole family particularly horrified the English, in whose Protestant view a murderer should die for his act.)

He pressed for a scorched earth policy in Ireland, noting that the destruction of crops and animals had been successful in crushing the Second Desmond Rebellion of which he was a part.

However in 1598, during the Nine Years War, Spenser was, ironically, driven from his home by the native Irish forces of Aodh Ó Néill. His castle at Kilcolman was burned

In 1599, Spenser travelled to London, where he died on January 13th at the age of forty-six. According to Ben Jonson, in another and tragic irony it was "for want of bread".

Edmund Spenser's coffin was carried to his grave in Westminster Abbey by other poets, who threw many pens and pieces of poetry into his grave followed with many tears.

His second wife, Elizabeth, survived him and went on to remarry twice.

Spenser was called a Poets' Poet and was admired by John Milton, William Blake, William Wordsworth, John Keats, Lord Byron, and Alfred Lord Tennyson, among others. Walter Raleigh wrote a dedicatory poem to The Faerie Queene in 1590, in which he claims to admire and value Spenser's work more so than any other in the English language. John Milton in his Areopagitica called Spenser "our sage and serious poet . . . whom I dare be known to think a better teacher than Scotus or Aquinas".

It is praise indeed and clearly shows why Edmund Spenser is indeed part of the Pantheon of our greatest Poets.

Edmund Spenser – A Concise Bibliography

1569 - Jan van der Noodt's A theatre for Worldlings, including poems translated into English by Spenser from French sources.

1579 - The Shepheardes Calender, published under the pseudonym "Immerito".

1580 - Three proper, and wittie, familar letters

1590 - The Faerie Queene, Books I–III

1591 - Complaints, Containing sundrie small Poemes of the Worlds Vanitie

1592 - Axiochus, a translation of a pseudo-Platonic dialogue from the original Ancient Greek; attributed to "Edw: Spenser" but the attribution is uncertain

1592 - Daphnaïda. An Elegy upon the death of the noble and vertuous Douglas Howard, Daughter and heire of Henry Lord Howard, Viscount Byndon, and wife of Arthure Gorges Esquier

1595 - Amoretti and Epithalamion

1595 - Astrophel. A Pastorall Elegie vpon the death of the most Noble and valorous Knight, Sir Philip Sidney.

1595 - Colin Clouts Come home againe

1596 - Four Hymns (poem)|Fowre Hymnes dedicated from the court at Greenwich.

1596 - Prothalamion

1596 - The Faerie Queene, Books IV-VI

1598 - A Veue of the Present State of Irelande (Manuscript)

1599 - Babel, Empress of the East – a dedicatory poem prefaced to Lewes Lewkenor's The Commonwealth of Venice.

1609 - Two Cantos of Mutabilitie published together with a reprint of The Fairie Queene.

1611 - First folio edition of Spenser's collected works

1633 - A Veue of the Present State of Irelande, a prose treatise on the reformation of Ireland.

www.ingramcontent.com/pod-product-compliance
Lightning Source LLC
Chambersburg PA
CBHW061445040426
42450CB00007B/1222